S0-BAG-942

WITHDRAWN

THE MULTICULTURAL STATES
OF
EAST AFRICA

Centre for Developing-Area Studies
McGill University
KEITH CALLARD LECTURES

I. THE ECONOMICS OF DEVELOPMENT IN SMALL COUNTRIES
WITH SPECIAL REFERENCE TO THE CARIBBEAN.
William G. Demas. 1965

II PROBLEMS AND PROSPECTS OF ECONOMIC INTEGRATION IN
WEST AFRICA. Nicolas G. Plessz. 1968

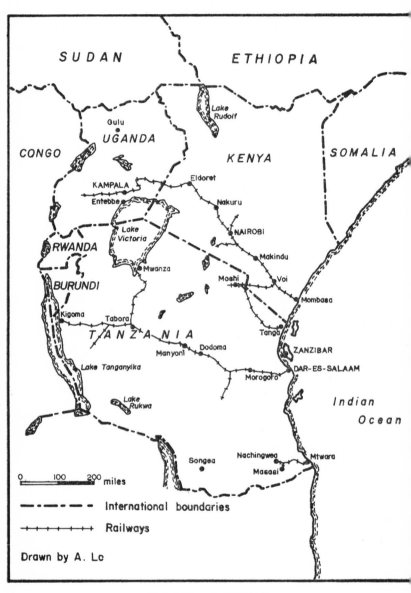

EAST AFRICA

Centre for Developing-Area Studies
McGill University
Keith Callard Lectures
Series III

THE MULTICULTURAL STATES
OF
EAST AFRICA

by
AUDREY I. RICHARDS

Montreal and London
PUBLISHED FOR THE CENTRE BY
MCGILL-QUEEN'S UNIVERSITY PRESS
1969

CARL A. RUDISILL LIBRARY
LENOIR RHYNE COLLEGE

© McGill-Queen's University Press 1969
Printed in Canada
by John Deyell Limited
SBN 7735-0067-7 (Cloth)
SBN 7735-0077-4 (Paper)
Library of Congress Catalog Card No. 74-101260

301. 29676
R 39 m
72731
Jan., 1971

This work has been published with the help of a grant from the Social Sciences Research Council of Canada using funds provided by the Canada Council.

FOREWORD

INDEPENDENCE came only a few short years ago to the
territories which had made up British East Africa. And
yet, the new states have already traced out complex lines
of economic and political development.

The record has naturally been shaped by the special
conditions and problems of each country. But it also
bears the imprint of forces common to the entire region
—and perhaps none more powerful than that of ethnic
diversity, or "multiculturalism." Drawing on her rich
East African experience, Dr. Audrey I. Richards uses this
theme to unlock some of the mysteries surrounding
the process of social change before and since independence.

In particular, she shows how multiculturalism in-
fluenced the colonial systems of public administration,
land tenure and local politics; also how it has coloured
the various rural development schemes undertaken in
the years since independence. An interesting case study
of Uganda reveals that intertribal tensions were accen-
tuated by independence, and that the ruling élites were
unwilling or unable to recognize the full reality of these
ethnic differences. But multiculturalism has had its in-
tegrative side too—as underscored by an incisive analysis
of the factors leading to national consciousness in
present-day East Africa.

More generally, Dr. Richards' book stimulates a host
of important questions that range far beyond her own
regional focus: What is the essence of "tribalism" in the

modern world? How does it affect the competition for office in the central governments of the new states, as well as the formation of political parties there? What are the difficulties involved in modernizing local government and rural agriculture in countries with marked group differences in language and political organization?

The author came very well equipped, indeed, to deliver these lectures on "The Multicultural States of East Africa"—the third Keith Callard Series sponsored by the McGill Centre for Developing-Area Studies. She has done extensive field research in Uganda and Zambia; and she has served as Director of the East African Institute of Social Research at Makerere University College, and also as Director of the Centre of African Studies at Cambridge University. In addition, she is a former President of the African Studies Association of the United Kingdom.

While Dr. Richards' stay at McGill was all too brief, it was much appreciated by staff and students alike. In fact, the Callard public lectures, her special seminars, her research consultation with interested McGill scholars—all this, and more, contributed heavily to the kind of atmosphere which makes the fall of 1966 well worth remembering, not only within the Centre but in the University at large.

IRVING BRECHER

Director
Centre for Developing-Area Studies

PREFACE

I HAD the honour to give these lectures in memory of Professor Keith B. Callard in October 1966. I have been much delayed in preparing them for publication and during that interval many important events have taken place in East Africa, and particularly in Uganda, with which my second lecture dealt. To take full account of these events would have meant a good deal of rewriting of the lectures; to avoid all reference to them would have given a somewhat unreal impression. I have compromised by adding a section to Chapter II describing the drastic changes which have taken place in Buganda and by making other additions in the form of footnotes.

A good deal of literature bearing on my subject has also appeared since then. I have not thought it proper to deal with this material in detail but I have made a few exceptions which I thought would add to the interest of my lectures. The report on a conference on rural development organized by the East African Program of the University of Syracuse with the cooperation of the Government of Tanzania was so relevant to the views I expressed in Chapter III that I have quoted from it quite extensively. I have also quoted from Professor July's book *History of Modern African Thought* (1967), and from *East Africa in Transition,* a set of essays edited by Stanley Diamond and F. Burke (1967).

My tardy production of this book is a poor return for the hospitality I received from McGill University during my visit and the kindness of the members of the Centre

for Developing-Area Studies, and of the Department of
Sociology and Anthropology. The help and companion-
ship I had during this, my first visit to Canada, made the
giving of the Keith Callard Lectures a memorable
experience.

CONTENTS

xi

M A P S

F I G U R E

CHAPTER I:
ETHNIC DIVERSITY IN THE
NEW EAST AFRICAN STATES

THE diversity of the peoples and cultures of Africa made an immediate impression on the travellers who first reached its shores. Nineteenth-century explorers certainly started their arduous expeditions because they wanted to map the geographical features of a continent that was then so little known. They hoped to follow new mountain ranges, to sail around lakes which then existed only in local rumour, or to look for the sources of great rivers such as the Nile or the Niger. But the diaries of these explorer-geographers show that they were fascinated by the differences in the appearance and behaviour of the peoples they met as well as, or perhaps even more than, by their environment. They began to sketch the inhabitants' clothing, their weapons and huts, their dances and ceremonies. In fact, many of these diaries are now valued more for their ethnographic material than for their descriptions of the physical features of a country which is no longer *terra incognita*.

The peoples the explorers encountered differed in appearance, behaviour, and settlement patterns, and this was immediately noted, if not always sketched. We now know that those ethnic groups also differed markedly in language although our explorers say little of their linguistic difficulties, probably because they used interpreters, mainly Swahili speakers in East Africa, and because

1

they usually stayed only a short time in each place. By contrast, our travellers tell us a good deal about what they call "the dispositions" of the peoples they met, who are described as being friendly, hostile, suspicious, avaricious, immoral, or savage. In other words, they all reacted differently to the arrival of the European and his caravan of porters! African people still react in different ways to foreigners and to their innovating schemes, and present-day travellers and development experts still explain these reactions in terms of the people's dispositions—their laziness, conservatism, or hatred of strangers —rather than in terms of their past history, their political and economic institutions, and their system of values, as we shall attempt to do here.

Our explorers also commented, even during the most fleeting of their halts, on the variety of systems of government among the peoples they met. The leaders of geographical expeditions naturally made contact with the local kings, chiefs, or elders on whom they were dependent for safe passage through a district, or for the organization of food supplies or canoes. But their descriptions of the courts and governments of the people they encountered show that they were not only concerned with the practical needs of their caravans. The differences between one group and another were striking enough to arouse the traveller's intellectual curiosity as well. Speke, moving slowly through South Uganda in 1862, evidently was struck by the political organization of Buganda, with its king, ministers, courtiers, and hierarchy of chiefs, its military and labour levies, and its system of taxation. He constantly compared these people with those he had seen en route from the coast. He was amazed at the size of the Ganda capital and wrote, "It was a magnificent sight. A whole hill covered with

2

gigantic huts, such as I had never seen in Africa before."[1]
Lonsdale, entering the federation of Ashanti kingdoms
in 1881 from an area where the political organization
was less elaborate, wrote "One is aware of having reached
a new country. A system of some kind impresses itself on
the senses."[2] European politicians and journalists have
tended, and still tend, to talk about *the* Africans or *the*
natives, but explorers and travellers did not make the
same mistake.

The professional anthropologists who began to make
intensive studies of African peoples from the 1930s onward showed that African political systems were even
more numerous and complex than the explorers had
imagined. The ethnic groups described by the anthropologists varied in size from the Ashanti and Ganda (each
nearly two million strong), and the Yoruba and Ibo,
who numbered over five million each in 1950, to the
smaller tribes such as the Amba of south-western Uganda
or the Mandari of the southern Sudan, who are reckoned
at about thirty thousand each, or the Hadza of Tanzania,
a hunting and collecting people, who number little more
than five hundred souls.

The political structures of these people have been
shown to range from loosely organized hunting bands
such as those of the Bushmen or Dorobo, or the extended family groups of nomadic pastoral peoples such
as the Turkana of Kenya or the pastoral Fulani of West
Africa, to the segmentary societies which split and keep
on splitting into a number of more or less autonomous
segments under their own clan elders, merely observing
some common law in war and blood revenge. The Nuer

[1] John Hanning Speke, *Journal of the Discovery of the Source of the
Nile* (Edinburgh and London: Blackwood and Sons, 1863), p. 283.

[2] Cited by Ivor Wilkes, in "Aspects in Bureaucratization in Ashanti in
the Nineteenth Century," *Journal of African History*, 7, no. 2 (1966): 215.

and other Nilotic peoples fall into this category. Margery Perham records that among the four million Ibo of south-eastern Nigeria, there were as many as two thousand autonomous political units in 1937.[3] Besides these, there are the African societies in which authority is wielded by groups of men of the same age who pass through life as members, successively, of a young warriors' set, an older warriors' set, and an elders' group, and who carry out their respective duties by means of a series of councils based on age. Some of the most famous tribes in East Africa, such as the Masai and the Kikuyu, fall into this category. Then there are of course the innumerable chiefdoms, kingdoms, federations, and empires which have appeared from time to time all over the continent. Some of these African states boasted long histories when the European travellers or administrators first arrived. The kabakas (or kings) of Buganda, for instance, trace their descent through thirty-five holders of the title. Some states, on the other hand, were conquest states quite recently formed, such as the polities of the conquering Fulani in Nigeria which established themselves as late as the mid-nineteenth century. Some, again, were tiny societies produced by the break-up of previous empires, like those of the numerous peoples in the Congo area.

Many powerful African kings with courts, ministers, and armies have passed into European history and fiction; Shaka of Zululand, Moshesh of Basutoland, Lobengula of Rhodesia, and the kings of Dahomey are cases in point. There are countless rulers who never came into such dramatic conflict with the European invaders, but whose systems of government achieved a com-

[3] Margery F. Perham, *Native Administration in Nigeria* (London: Oxford University Press, 1937), p. 222.

4

plexity that fascinated the visiting anthropologist, and later, the political scientist.

The questions discussed in this study spring directly from the cultural and structural diversity of the African peoples. Do these traditional polities, some small, some large, still survive within the modern independent states of Africa, or do they remain merely hunting grounds for the assiduous Ph.D., the historian, the sociologist, or the political scientist? If the tribal societies survive, what makes these groups conscious of their identity, proud of it, and unwilling to merge it in a larger whole? Under what conditions has the coming of independence swept away ethnic rivalries or, alternatively, strengthened intertribal hostilities or even created new ones? Which types and combinations of traditional political systems have made the formation of a centralized government easy and which difficult? It is clear that in many parts of Africa what was the wonder of the explorer and the social laboratory of the anthropologist has proved a problem, and often a nearly insoluble problem, to the constitution-makers and to the central governments of the new states.

THE ETHNIC GROUPS OF EAST AFRICA

Each new African government had a different hand to play when it reached independence. The number of tribes in each territory varied, both in their absolute size and, a very important point, in their size relative to each other. Their history, economic development, and opportunities for progress differed, as did their political structure. These are significant factors. It is commonly said, for instance, that Tanzania has no tribal problem whereas Uganda and Kenya have. How can we account

5

for the difference? As a basis for an answer, I shall discuss some of the characteristic features of the ethnic situation in the East African context.

To begin, the population of East Africa is much less dense that that of West Africa. Tanzania with 9.2 million inhabitants has a population density of 40.2 per square mile; Kenya with 6.9 million has a density of 28.7; Uganda with 6.7 million people has a population density of 94.6 per square mile.[4] It is true that in a dispersed population, powerful African kingdoms which resent amalgamation with other kingdoms tend to be rare, and therefore we might think that it would be easier to form centralized modern states in countries where the people are widely scattered. But at the other end of the scale there is the tribalism of isolation to be reckoned with. Isolation limits a man to a very small world. When I was working in the northern province of Zambia from 1930 to 1934, the first plane to land in the district came down at a crude bush airport. It was a forerunner of what was to become a regular London to Capetown service. The three Europeans present stood commenting on the wonder of the opening up of Africa, but members of the local tribe, the Bemba, ran up shouting, "What an extraordinary thing! Some white men have come down from the sky and they say they have never heard of us, the Bemba!" They were a hundred and fifty thousand strong, poor, under-developed, four hundred miles from the nearest railhead: but they had the ethnocentrism of isolation, a phenomenon more common in East than in West Africa before the coming of independent rule.

4 See East African Common Services Organization, East African Statistical Department, *Quarterly Economic and Statistical Review* (Nairobi: Government Printer, June, 1964).

The settlement patterns of the East also differ from those of the West. East Africa is characterized by the number of its small dispersed villages, homesteads of a man and his married sons or hamlets of two to three hundred people, whereas West Africa tends to be a region of large indigenous towns such as those of the Ashanti and the Yoruba or of the Northern Emirates. Regular trade routes across the Sahara linked the coastal centres of West Africa with the Mediterranean from the fifteenth century onward, and markets and marketing are ancient institutions there. Urban life and a system of external trade naturally put people of different origins in contact. Anyone who has stood in one of the great indigenous markets of West Africa, such as Kaduna, Benin, Kumasi, or Accra, will have vivid memories of the medley of men and women of different races and tribal groups who regularly mix there. In East Africa, by contrast, the journey from the coast to the interior was hard and the prizes of such trade less rewarding. The Arabs reached Uganda and the interior of Tanzania only in the middle of the nineteenth century.

In its ethnic composition, East Africa is characterized by its large number of small tribes: 120 in Tanzania, 31 in Uganda, and 27 in Kenya. Many of these tribes number only 150,000 to 200,000, and the only groups which reach anything like the size of the Ashanti, the Ibo, or the Yoruba are the Kikuyu speakers or the Ganda, reckoned at about two million people each. The latter is an important fact to note. As we shall see, the presence of ethnic groups which are large in relation to the other constituent groups in a new state has often been a cause of rivalry, tension, and even attempts at separatism.

The indigenous people of East Africa are divided into four main language groups, a cultural difference which

7

obviously affects the possibilities of integration in its three major states, Kenya, Uganda, and Tanzania. The Bantu speakers are the largest group. In 1938, Lord Hailey estimated their number at forty million in Africa as a whole.[5] They cover an enormous area south of a line that runs from the Nigeria-Cameroons frontier, across the Congo region and Uganda, to the hinterland of Mombasa. They stretch from the territory of the Great Lakes to Cape Province and thus include the majority of the inhabitants of Tanzania and South Uganda, as well as a large and important enclave in Kenya, mainly Kikuyu. Bantu languages have a characteristic structure with nouns divided into ten or more classes with appropriate prefixes attached. They are thus easily recognizable. The languages of the Bantu speakers resemble each other as closely as do French, Italian, and Spanish.

The Nilotic peoples are much less numerous, about three million strong. They inhabit the Nile Valley, West Uganda, and the West Nyanza province of Kenya. The Nilotic languages are entirely different from those of the Bantu, as different, perhaps, as Italian and German.

The third ethnic division, commonly described as Nilo-Hamitic, is a small one. The pastoral peoples of Northern Kenya and Uganda belong to this group, as well as some small tribes in North Tanzania. The Nilo-Hamitic peoples, such as the Masai and Turkana, speak a language of Hamitic type. There are also the peoples properly called Hamitic, that is to say, the pastoral peoples of the Kenyan border with Ethiopia and Somaliland such as the Boran and Somali.

In East Africa, in the years before independence, there were also larger concentrations of immigrants from

5 Lord Hailey, *An African Survey* (London: Oxford University Press, 1938), p. 20.

Europe and Asia than there were in West or Central Africa. In Kenya, Uganda, and Tanzania, for instance, there were the following numbers of immigrants of different types according to the census figures in Table 1.[6]

TABLE 1

IMMIGRANTS TO EAST AFRICA

Country	Europeans	Asians	Arabs	Other non-natives*	Africans
Kenya (1959)	66,400	169,600	37,100	964	6,171,000
Tanzania (1957)	20,534	71,660	19,088	7,014	8,662,684
Uganda (1959)	10,866	69,103	1,946	4,164	6,449,558

*Including Goans

These great language divisions obviously raise practical problems for those engaged in nation-building. They are often overlooked by visiting experts from overseas who speak English and mainly to the educated African élite. Nilotic and Bantu languages have neither structure nor vocabulary in common. The provision of common textbooks for primary schools has always been a difficulty in countries, such as Kenya and Uganda, where there are tribes belonging to both language groups. The formation of a common, as distinct from a tribal, civil service at the rural level encounters the same obstacle. In colonial days, European district officers complained of being moved from areas where they had learned the vernacular to ones where it was unfamiliar. A Bantu civil servant moving to a Nilotic or Nilo-Hamitic area is in much the

[6] E. Hopkins, "Racial Minorities in British East Africa," in *The Transformation of East Africa,* ed. Stanley Diamond and Fred G. Burke (New York: Basic Books, 1966), p. 84.

same position and often equally unwilling to keep learning new languages.

Swahili has been used as an administrative lingua franca in Kenya and Tanzania and has been taught as a second language in schools. Since independence, it has been made the language of instruction in primary schools; it is the simplest form of Bantu and can be learned from a variety of textbooks. Swahili is a language with an ancient history; it was used by the first explorers and traders. Africans, both men and women, use it to communicate with strangers from other ethnic groups both in Kenya and Tanzania. The different Indian communities are usually able to use Swahili as well as English. European administrators often learned classical Swahili while other Europeans—settlers, labour officers, and housewives—spoke what might be called "kitchen" Swahili, contemptuously referred to as "Kisettler" or "the language of the settlers" in Kenya. Though Swahili was not perhaps a colloquial language in the colonial era, it was the language of administration, commerce, and intertribal communication, and it has certainly been an asset to the modern political leaders of Kenya and Tanzania with their eyes fixed on some kind of East African federation. In Uganda, however, Swahili is disliked by the dominant Ganda whose language, Luganda, was taught in schools all over the area in the early days of the British Protectorate and therefore might have become the lingua franca of the Protectorate. Ganda continue to conduct all their administrative and legal business in their own language and are proud of doing so. In fact, the language has become one of the important symbols of their ethnic distinction.

English is taught in the higher forms of the primary schools all over East Africa, and it is used as the medium of instruction in the secondary schools and universities. To many Europeans it seems obvious that English should be the lingua franca of the whole region, and they cannot understand why it should not have been accepted as such already. There are many practical difficulties. In villages where English reading matter is scarce and contact with Europeans infrequent, the people quickly return to their own language. Swahili is an easier "foreign" language for a Bantu speaker than English. Also inter-tribal rivalry may make the vernacular language a symbol, as in Buganda, and then the educated élite begin to use it generally as a medium of communication. In 1954, when the Kabaka of Buganda was deported by the Protectorate government and Buganda felt threatened, newspapers written in Luganda, not English, were numerous. In 1965, when Buganda again felt threatened, this time by the dominance of the Nilotic and Nilo-Hamitic politicians of North Uganda in the National Assembly and in the central civil service, the people expressed themselves in a linguistic idiom saying, "We won't be dominated by the O's"—"O" being the common linguistic prefix of Nilotic names, much like the "Mac" of Scottish names. Well-known leaders such as Obote, the President of Uganda, O'cheng, or Odinga fall into this category.

Differences in traditional political structure, have also proved divisive factors in the East African situation. If I were to say that the Bantu peoples were organized into chiefdoms, the Nilo-Hamites along age-set lines, and the Nilotics on the basis of segmentary lineages, anthropologists would protest. There are of course exceptions to such a generalization. For example, the Gisu and Kiga of Uganda are Bantu speakers but they have a segmentary structure, and the Kikuyu speak a Bantu language but are organized in age-sets and do not acknowledge chiefs. But this rough generalization ilustrates why, during the colonial period, a great variety of traditional authorities had to be developed further to meet the differences in these political systems, and the amalgamation of chief-doms with acephalous societies proved difficult.

Each type of political structure is inevitably associated with a different set of political values. People who have been brought up in a chiefdom tend to despise those who have lived under a less centralized form of government. In Uganda, for instance, the peoples of the kingdom of Buganda condemn the segmentary Nilotic peoples to the north as lawless, disorganized, and savage; the Nilotics, for their part, tend to scorn the centralized government of Buganda with its traditional hierarchy of officials, and to accuse the Ganda of crawling on their bellies in front of their chiefs from dawn to dusk. In the present circumstances, the acephalous peoples, whether of segmentary or age-set structure, claim that they are more "democratic" than their neighbours who belong to chiefdoms, and that therefore they are more "western" and modern in outlook. This they claim, even if they have not yet reached as high a standard of literacy as the citizens of some of the kingdoms they affect to despise. Mutual frustration and irritation results. This is merely one example of the extent to which tribal structure, and therefore tribal values, still influences the present-day relations of a number of ethnic groups in East Africa.

By contrast, traditional religious beliefs have not proved divisive factors in this region. Ancestor worship takes many forms throughout the area but there is a common basis of belief underlying it. Spasmodic disputes over the ownership of local shrines occur from time to time, especially where one group has conquered the area held by another, but I do not remember a case of one tribe being seriously embroiled with another because of cult differences. It is the universal, imported religions, such as Christianity and Mohammedanism, which have been the basis of serious conflicts, partly no doubt because they take a man away from his cult of family and kinship gods and align him with a group of adherents of a new faith which is outside family and locality and often outside the tribe. The warfare in Buganda between the converts to Catholicism, Protestantism, and Islam, which rent the country at the end of the nineteenth century, is a case in point.

Apart from language and political structure, the many other cultural differences between the peoples of East Africa—differing descent systems, patrilineal or matrilineal; different forms of family organization, economic activities, or ceremonies—need not have made integration difficult. But of course, as in the case of language, such ethnic differences may become symbols of tribal identity when a people feels threatened with obliteration. Ganda men who had worn European dress all their lives donned the long white Arab shirt or *kanzu,* and even the traditional bark-cloth, when they felt outraged by the deportation of their king in 1954. Educated as well as uneducated Kikuyu fought for the retention of their female circumcision ceremonies when these were prohibited by European government officials and missionaries.

THE PERSISTENCE OF TRIBAL SOCIETIES

What has made African peoples so fearful of their obliteration as groups? In each of the territories with which we are concerned the people had been under the rule of a central government—though a foreign one—

13

for over sixty years, when independence was declared. The Kenya highlands were separated from Uganda in 1902, and the territory known as Kenya Colony was created and remained in this form until independence was granted in 1963. In Uganda, the rule of the Protectorate government lasted sixty-eight years, from the proclamation of the Protectorate over Buganda in 1894 until Independence Day in 1962. In Tanzania, German rule was established in 1889; the country passed under a British Mandate after World War I, and under United Nations Trusteeship after World War II. These are much shorter periods of European rule than those established in West Africa, but sixty to seventy years might well have been long enough to obliterate tribal polities if the colonial government had had sufficient staff and resources, and if either the British or the Africans had so desired at the time.

We have discussed some of the cultural differences among the peoples of East Africa, particularly differences in language and political values. But I do not believe that such differences are the main causes of the fierce determination of some African tribes to remain distinct and apart. Territorial segregation and forms of corporate ownership of land, the type of political administration adopted by the colonial power, and the history and traditions of political dominance of one tribe over another seem to me to be more significant factors. To these we shall have to add the new inequalities, particularly economic inequalities, which created new forms of ethnic rivalry after the granting of independent rule.

In East Africa, the most common form of customary land tenure was one which identified a territory with a single ethnic group. Land was theoretically the property of the tribe or its chief. Those who cultivated it, or

14

grazed it, did so by virtue of being members of the tribe, subjects of its chief, or members of a lineage with corporate rights over the land. Land could not be bought or sold by individuals. An outsider who wanted a plot of land to cultivate had to become a tribesman by making an act of homage to the chief, or by being incorporated in a local lineage by some genealogical fiction. A tribesman who spent half his life in a town many miles from his home still maintained the right to land in the rural area in which he was born by virtue of his membership in the group. This tied him effectively to his tribal unit. Nothing would have more quickly destroyed the sense of tribal unity in Africa than the introduction of individual freehold over land, with rights of sale to members belonging to any and all ethnic groups in the territory. But it is also true that nothing would have produced so strong a sense of insecurity among peasants who were used to the traditional occupier tenancy based on tribal affiliation. If their small plots could have been purchased by the highest bidder, many would have found themselves landless and often without alternative employment, and they would have resented the large fortunes made by their fellow-tribesmen who had speculated shrewdly in the purchase of land. Today this resentment is felt in any part of East Africa where land speculation exists.

Most ethnic groups or "tribes" had become units of local administration during the sixty or seventy years of colonial rule in East Africa. Traditional authorities, whether chiefs, headmen, or clan elders, had been legally recognized and given new functions. Traditional councils and courts of law were also given statutory powers. "Chiefs in Council," or in some cases, councils themselves, were recognized as "native authorities." Local officials, clerks, accountants, and agricultural and health inspectors tended to be recruited from within the same tribal unit. This method of colonial administration through traditional authorities—the famous system of "indirect rule"—was characteristic of British rule in Africa until after World War II. It obviously made for the perpetuation of diverse African polities, although it had many initial advantages as a system of colonial administration. It has been much criticized by African politicians and by political scientists, particularly perhaps by those from America, but it is doubtful whether any other policy would have been as successful in the early days of British rule in Africa.

A colonial power which wants to enforce law and order in a backward area and then to introduce the fundamental social services surely has only three possibilities open to it. First, it can rule through its own nationals at all levels of government: at the centre, in the provinces, counties, subcounties, and villages (see Figure 1, p. 21), and it can introduce its own institutions of government by force. Such a policy would have produced a unified civil service under a central government and would have obliterated tribal polities, with the maximum initial opposition from the people. But, in fact, no colonial power in Africa—Belgian, French, German, Portuguese, or British—has been able to administer all levels of government by means of it own nationals, because of the expense of employing such an enormous number of expatriate staff. At the beginning of colonial rule, the number of British administrators in each of the East African territories could have been counted on the fingers of two hands, if not one. Lugard had a company of Sudanese troops when he arrived in Uganda in 1890, and from that date until the arrival of Sir Harry

16

Johnston in 1897, there seem to have been ten British officers in the country, of whom three were killed, one died of illness, and one was invalided home. Direct rule was, practically speaking, an impossibility in those days.

The second alternative for a colonial power was the use of African agents trained for colonial requirements. There were few literate Africans available at the time but it still would have been possible to appoint men loyal to the colonial government rather than to the tribal authorities of the area in which they were working. This was the policy followed by the Germans in most parts of Tanganyika when they appointed Arabs or Swahilis as subordinates to each expatriate district officer. These were the *Akidas,* the government agents, whom Hailey describes as efficient but hampered by the fact that they knew only Moslem law, not tribal law, and that they were much disliked by the local people for their over-bearing ways.[7] In Uganda, the temporary use of Ganda chiefs to administer the Soga, the Lango, the Teso, and the Kiga, who had less-developed political institutions, was a similar experiment in the use of African agents. It was an experiment which lasted only a few years in each instance and it was an unpopular method of government in most cases. If it had persisted, it might well have produced a united Uganda with a single civil service, but it would have meant a Ganda empire over subject tribes and not a union of equal peoples.

Another variant of the African-agent solution was that adopted in Kenya. This colonial government had to deal with age-set societies ruled by a series of councils at the junior warrior, senior warrior, and elder levels. A government memorandum of 1935 states that "the

[7] Lord Hailey, *An African Survey,* rev. ed. (London: Oxford University Press, 1957), p. 472.

political organisation of government before the British occupation was of a very nebulous character."[8] It was not of course nebulous to the people concerned. In fact, the membership and procedures of its age-based councils seem to have been rather clearly defined, but it was difficult for an alien government to recognize and use them. The British administration therefore appointed African headmen, who were given power over areas called "locations" (1912) and who, by 1925, were officially, though rather misleadingly, described as "chiefs."

These African officials were directly appointed by the government, though local opinion was consulted and, later, chiefs were chosen from a set of names submitted to public meetings. These men were not traditional leaders but "a native administration service." Thus Kenya was never an indirect-rule area in the usual sense of the word; but it must be remembered that all the larger ethnic groups such as the Kikuyu, Kamba, and Masai were still administered as separate units and by African civil servants belonging to their own tribe.

The third alternative open to a colonial power with small resources in men and money was to recognize and support the indigenous political authorities but to change their functions and to modernize their institutions (that is, indirect rule).[9] It was a system based on Lugard's experience of ruling through the powerful emirs and their traditional administrations in Northern Nigeria. In East Africa, the recognition of the Bantu kings of South Uganda, and of Buganda, Bunyoro, Toro, and Ankole by special treaties, was tantamount to an acceptance of indirect rule, though the term was not in use. In North, East, and West Uganda, after the brief

8 *Ibid.*, p. 446.
9 See above, pp. 15-16

period of rule by Ganda chiefs, the Nilotic and Nilo-Hamitic tribes in these regions as well as the segmentary Bantu peoples were also recognized as separate units of government. In Tanganyika, indirect rule was introduced in 1926 by Sir Donald Cameron.[10] Kenya followed a somewhat different path, as we have seen, but one which still retained the distinctions between the major tribal units.

In the years between the two world wars, indirect rule ceased to be merely a matter of practical necessity and became a creed and the focus of many fervent hopes and endeavours. It was viewed as the means by which each small tribal unit would be allowed to follow its own institutions and customs and would no longer be dragooned into acceptance of British ideas of local government. Indirect rule became a philosophy, but it was also the name given to a policy of phased development in the African colonies. Tribal dignitaries were to be educated in modern systems of local government. They were to be supported by officers trained in new skills: accountancy, clerical work, agricultural practices, and school and health inspection. Tribal councils were to be altered in composition so that educated members would have an increasingly dominant part to play in local government; new elected elements were finally to displace the hereditary ones. Ethnic groups too small to be efficient units of local government were to be amalgamated. Tribal councils were to be united into regional councils, and these were to be represented, in time, on a central legislature. According to the dreams of the British administrators of the time, a unified state would thus be created out of a polycultural, polyglot population.

10 Tanganyika, Laws of Tanganyika, *Native Authorities Ordinance, 1926*, cap. 47, 1928.

This final stage was never reached in the East African territories, but it is worth pausing a moment to see how far tribal substructures remained distinct at the time independence was declared. A simple diagram illustrates the problems the new African states had to face.

In Figure 1, the *A*s, the *B*s, and the *C*s are tribal units. Their peoples differ in language, culture, and structure. *A* is depicted here as a chiefdom of a pyramid type with a paramount chief or king and subordinate chiefs under him; the *B*s are a segmentary people with a gazetted native authority consisting of clan elders; while the *C*s are a series of small chiefdoms united in a federation with a central council.

Our three groups probably spoke three different languages, and they represented three different types of political structure. Each "native authority" had, in the period under discussion, its own sphere of executive action. It made decisions in councils which had statutory powers at the primary, secondary, and perhaps tertiary levels; such councils were given control over an increasing number of local social services such as roads, water supplies, agricultural extension work, or primary schools. It collected taxes, usually retaining a fixed portion for local use, while remitting the rest to the central government. It drew up its budget, had its own staff of administrators, clerks, and inspectors. The sphere of action of the traditional authorities had been completely changed by the colonial power, but the tribal microcosms remained, for the most part, intact.

Besides its executive powers, the native authority had its statutory law courts and administered its own customary law in cases involving, for example, marriage and the family, or offences against property and person.

ADMINISTRATIVE PYRAMID IN A PROVINCE IN A COLONIAL TERRITORY IN EAST AFRICA

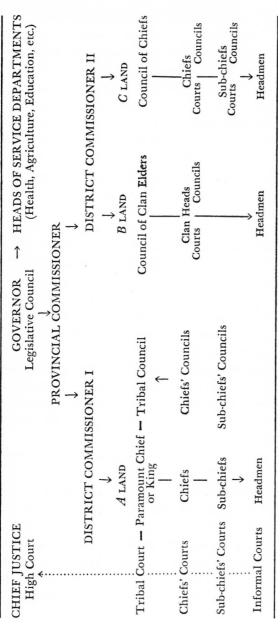

The POSTS filled by expatriate staff are indicated by capital letters.
A land is a political unit consisting of a tribal chiefdom with a paramount chief or king, chiefs, and sub-chiefs.
B land is a segmentary society with a council of clan elders appointed by the British.
C land is occupied by a federation of chiefdoms united in a council of chiefs.

Below these statutory courts at the primary and secondary level, there were commonly informal courts, unrecognized by the colonial government and functioning much as they must have done before British rule. White administrators supervised the statutory courts, taught the keeping of records, enforced British rules of evidence, and heard cases such as murder and witchcraft, over which the native courts had no jurisdiction. Cases went on appeal through various lower courts to the High Court of the territory, where a British judge presided. It is important to try to visualize the variety of legal microcosms so maintained. A set of customary rules might apply to some one hundred and fifty thousand people, while different legal concepts governed the decisions of the courts in the neighbouring tribe. In a patrilineal area, for instance, the children would be given to the father, or to his lineage, in the case of divorce; while a few miles away in the courts of a different, and in this case matrilineal, people, the children would be allotted to the mother and her brothers.

In the case of a large ethnic group, the British District Commissioner would become immersed in the affairs of a particular tribe which was both a unit of common culture and also a unit of political and legal administration. He would be referred to as an expert on the As or the Bs. In other districts he might have groups of very diverse cultures under his care and might therefore have to administer peoples speaking different languages.

Figure 1 shows two things. First, under this system all senior officials whether at the district, provincial, or central level were British, until the years immediately before independence when rapid Africanization took place. Second, it is clear that although the system provided for vertical links connecting the village, the subdistrict, district, and province with the central government, there were few horizontal links between the different native authorities. The figure does not, and cannot, show the number of Africans who participated in their own local government by this system of indirect rule and who thereby received some kind of training in modern methods of administration. Nor does it show the extent to which the administrative pyramid relied on the services of thousands of unpaid traditional dignitaries at the village level, the base of the pyramid.

Here, then, were two factors making for the persistence of African subcultures: tribal ownership of land and therefore a measure of tribal segregation, and an administrative policy which recognized tribal political institutions as units of local government. There is a third factor which might be loosely described as political values, in the sense of political traditions and symbols, and group rituals. Some African peoples have lively traditions of historical splendour; this is particularly true in the case of kingdoms and other well-integrated polities. Memories of successful conquest of neighbouring peoples make a tribe most unwilling to contemplate a position of equality with those they conquered, as the history of Uganda shows. Unifying symbols such as a king, or common rituals such as the initiation ceremonies of the Gisu or the various age-set ceremonies of many of the Kenya tribes, also make or made African groups feel that they are unique and different from their neighbours. Many of them wished to remain so.

Some integrating factors for people belonging to these different subcultures in the years immediately preceding independence can be listed briefly here. One unifying feature is British institutions introduced into East Africa many years earlier. Both Catholic and Protestant missions held congresses attended by delegates from all over the territory, bringing together men and women of different tribes. Higher education was also an integrating factor. Secondary schools and, later, universities used English as the medium of instruction and drew their scholars from a wide area. Makerere College, the East African university-to-be, was an institution which drew African students not only from the three East African territories and Zanzibar, but also from Zambia and Malawi. Old students' reunions and circulating letters still keep some sense of unity among Makerere graduates even though Makerere became a University College in 1963, and now draws its students mainly from Uganda. The Royal College at Nairobi and the University of Tanzania also became University Colleges for their own territories.

The cities of East Africa, few as they were, grew rapidly and attracted men and women of all ethnic groups for industrial and other employment and for higher education. Forty tribes were represented in Kampala and Nairobi, and over forty-seven in Dar-es-Salaam. Small tribal settlements formed wherever city dwellers were able to put up their own houses.[11] In African towns, there are also tribal associations for social and welfare purposes and for recreation. They seem to be especially numerous in Nairobi. Yet at the élite level the towns, here as in other parts of the world, tended to form a culture of their own which was not based in the main on tribal affiliation. The chief integrating force in each

[11] As distinct from being housed on council estates or locations in which houses were allocated in order of application and not by tribal affiliation. See Peter C. W. Gutkind, "Urban Conditions in Africa," *The Town Planning Review*, 32, no. 1 (1961): 20-32, for a description of the settlements in Kampala.

East African territory of course was this élite, composed of men and women who had become divorced from their tribal life through education or occupation and had adopted, or tried to adopt, British standards of living in clothing, housing, furniture, and entertainment. The small British minority was very definitely the reference group in each of these territories, even in times of bitter hostility to British rule. The élite disliked the thought of village life and, at that time, identified progress and civilization with British culture. In this they were at one with the British themselves. Though the latter admired "noble savages," they did not think it possible for an African to hold a high post unless he spoke English and could "eat with a knife and fork," the symbol of European culture in this context. The élite, with their almost slavish admiration of the British way of life, caused many a patronizing smile at the time. They were laughed at as "carbon copies." But in fact, the adoption of British culture was the only way in which they could achieve high-status positions. It was also through the colonial government that the Africans gained access to the greater world overseas which they so much valued. It gave them access to authorities in Great Britain, to its Christian churches, to the Anti-slavery Society and Aborigines Protection Society, to Members of Parliament, to the Prime Minister, the archbishops, or the monarch—and all these contacts were constantly used. Thus the African élite in these years was united by a British type of education, an inordinate desire for a British way of life, and their hopes of help from British authority figures.[12] They were united in their acceptance of a Western value

[12] Later, of course, in the United Nations and many other international bodies.

25

system since it was the only one they had in common, but after independence they had to struggle to find a distinct African personality or *présence.*

Finally, there were some special features of East African states as a whole during the postwar years. Colonies are inevitably plural societies in the sense that there must be at least two groups with different political structures, that of the indigenous people and that of the colonial power. But the situation in the East African colonies was more complex because of the number of tribal substructures and the sizeable Asian minorities. Michael G. Smith, in his description of the West Indies situation, distinguishes between "social plurality," the existence of separate systems of groups and relations,[13] and "cultural pluralism," the existence of separate norms, activities, and material culture producing cultural heterogeneity.[14] I make somewhat the same distinction when I describe the East African states as multistructural and multicultural.

The British in East Africa had no deep attachment to the land as had the indigenous people, except for the white settlers in the Kenya Highlands (which was virtually a European reserve), and some of the white settlers, German and English, in Tanzania. The structure of the British ruling groups was distinct in that its political institutions were modified British models exported to East Africa. The governors, with their plumed helmets for crowns, their enormous government houses for palaces, their uniformed outriders for guards, represented the British monarch. The legislative assemblies were described as "daughters" of their mother at West-

---

13 Michael G. Smith, *The Plural Society in the British West Indies* (Berkeley: University of California Press, 1965), p. 79.
14 *Ibid.,* p. 85.

minster even though they were not fully elected bodies until the 1960s. British law was administered in British-style courts. The British civil service practices were exported along with a British-style army and police. I call this a distinct political structure because Asians and Africans were absorbed into it only by adopting British-type roles, and then only as subordinates, during these years.

British culture as exported to the colonies was a very homogeneous one. In the economic field, the colonists formed mainly a high-income group, employed in the senior posts in the government services, in missionary work, and in industry. Apart from the small areas of European settlement, British immigrants took little part in agriculture and lived mostly in towns, often in housing "zoned" on racial lines and not facilitating contact with other groups. Standards of housing, furnishing, and entertaining were very uniform, chiefly because British civil servants were recruited predominately from the professional middle class and were usually the product of British public schools. Missionaries did not always come from this class, nor did British technicians, but the incomes of the latter were so high in relation to their earnings in their home country that the majority quickly adopted a standard of living something like that of the higher civil servants.

The British inhabitants of East Africa were part of one social network in towns. They had their own clubs and "tribal associations," which celebrated St. George's, St. Andrew's, and St. David's days. Asians and Africans belonged to different networks. The British were intent on introducing many elements of their own culture to Africans, such as their religion, political ideas, educational system, and ideas of health and nutrition, and claimed that this was their justification for colonizing. Curiously enough, they did not attempt to alter the culture of the Asians, who for the most part had their own schools and retained their own culture. The number of Hindu or Moslem Asians in East Africa converted to Christianity must have been negligible.

The Asian immigrants, like the African inhabitants but unlike the British, belonged to many subcultures. They came mainly from the Gujarati province of India, though there were some Sikhs and Pakistanis. H. S. Morris estimates that, in 1952, 57 per cent of those considered Asians were Hindus. These were divided into a number of castes, still mainly but not entirely endogamous and often looking for wives from India and not from local groups. About 43 per cent were Moslems. Although they were all reckoned "Indians" by both Europeans and Africans, their subcultures were very distinct, as Morris points out. Their social networks were usually separate and they practiced their own religious rites. The Moslems were themselves divided. For instance, in Uganda alone, 59 per cent of the Asians were Hindu, while 33 per cent were Moslems divided into the Shia and Sunni sects.[15] None of the Asian groups seem to have been proselytizing cultures. Most of the African Moslems derived their religion from much earlier Arab contacts and had their own mosques in Kampala.

In the economic field, the Asians were rarely attached to the land except in the case of a few plantations scattered throughout East Africa. They seldom did manual work in agriculture or industry. They were prominent in the business communities of the three territories and sometimes had their own Asian Chambers of Commerce.

15 H. S. Morris, *The Indians in Uganda* (Chicago: University of Chicago Press, 1968), pp. 12-15.

At one time Asians controlled the ginning and marketing of cotton in Uganda. They entered the middle ranks
of the government services. Many of them belonged to
the high-income groups of East Africa but could hardly
be said to belong to its upper and middle class, since
they never achieved high social prestige. Africans disliked them, since Asians held the intermediate jobs to
which they aspired, although the British felt it their
duty to advance the Africans in preference to the Indians.

Politically, Asians had no specific substructures as had
Africans, though they had a separate political status and,
at one time, separate representation in the central legislature. The Asian community did not form any strong
and separate political parties. They could be described
as a multicultural group without separate political institutions and holding an intermediate position between
African and European occupations and income.

Thus, the Africans formed both multicultural and
multistructural groups; the minority achieved high
status by becoming honorary Europeans with an élite
unified by an acceptance of Western values. The majority were peasant cultivators of countries dependent on
the export of primary produce, unskilled labourers, and
lower civil servants. The East African population of the
1950s was therefore distinguished by a British mono-
culture with multicultural Asian and African communities, the latter also being recognized as political substructures. It was economically differentiated, but the
three racial groups could hardly be described as a hier-
archal class system as is said to exist in the West Indies,
for example, since political views dominated economic
ones, in some instances, and the low-income Africans
often had a higher social status than the wealthier
Asians.

The common political symbols were the imperial ones: the British monarch's portrait on the walls of every native-authority headquarters, however small, and the Union Jack ritually struck at sundown at Government House and at each out-station. A national legislature, which might have become both an instrument of central government and its symbol, did not come into being as a fully elected parliament in any of the three East African territories until just before independence: in Kenya and Tanzania in 1960, and in Uganda in 1961.

CHAPTER II:
INDEPENDENCE AND THE NEW ETHNIC RIVALRIES: UGANDA AS A CASE STUDY

THE REJECTION OF THE TRIBE AS A POLITICAL UNIT

THE previous chapter described the multicultural, multistructural societies of East Africa in the years before World War II. After the war there was, for many reasons, a strong reaction against the tribe as a unit of local government. The Colonial Office virtually abandoned its philosophy of indirect rule. The development and integration of indigenous political institutions seemed much too slow as a preparation for independent government in East African territories, and independence seemed to be on the horizon, if not nearer. In any case, tribal organizations had collapsed in the rapidly growing towns and their suburbs, and some new form of local government for these areas seemed urgently needed. The Secretary of State, in his famous dispatch of 1947, urged colonial governments to create new local government organs to replace or supplement the native authorities;[1] these organs were to follow the British model rather than a series of tribal ones. African officials to be trained in higher standards of local administration were sent to the United Kingdom for special courses and were attached to British local authorities in that country to gain practical experience. Later, when courses in the field of local administration were developed at

[1] Great Britain, Secretary of State, *Despatch on Local Government*, Colonial Despatch, February 25, 1947.

Makerere University College and at special institutes for practical training in Kenya, Tanzania, and Uganda, the instruction was given mainly by experts in British local government. One could almost hear the sigh of relief that went up from countless colonial administrators when they realized that it was no longer necessary for them to try to understand the many and complex political institutions of the African peoples for whom they were responsible. From now on, it was "Buy British" as far as local government was concerned.

Later, the introduction of universal suffrage in every East African territory seemed to promise the integration of the various political structures by means of a British-type parliament. Tanzania had her first elected National Assembly in 1960 and an independent government the same year; Kenya had her National Assembly in 1961 and independence in 1963, while Uganda reached the same position in 1962, and independence in the same year.

Meanwhile, African societies, so long studied only by anthropologists, administrators, and missionaries, began to attract the attention of other social scientists. From about 1950 on, political scientists, mainly from America, began to make visits and research trips to African territories. They were interested in the exciting emergence of the new independent states, the evolution of central governments, and the introduction of universal franchise, rather than in local government. In the case of East Africa where, as we have seen, there was a multiplicity of small ethnic groups, their impatience with tribal loyalties and tribal identification was natural. Economists who were summoned in such large numbers to advise on African development during the same postwar period were also strong defenders of large political regions rather than smaller ones. Experts convinced of the economic advantages of an East African federation naturally looked askance at any evidence of tribal separatism or even tribal sentiment.

African politicians too were afraid of the persistence of tribal loyalties. They knew they would not be granted independence unless they solved their ethnic differences. It will be remembered that the independence of Kenya and Uganda was actually postponed for considerable periods until some compromise between tribal interests had been reached in these territories. It was natural that these politicians tended, and tend, to deny the cultural and structural differences which exist between the peoples that constitute the new states; indeed, it may be the policy of political parties to refuse to recognize them. In Tanzania, for instance, it is apparently an insult to ask a man to which tribe he belongs.

Educated Africans also tended to equate "tribalism" with barbarism and backwardness, and to view it as a stage through which people pass and leave behind permanently. They naturally wanted to dissociate themselves from the then-current image of a tribal Africa inhabited by witchdoctors, illiterate and retrograde chiefs, and men and women dancing around tom-toms. European journalists used and still use the word "tribalism" in somewhat the same way, and refer to it as though it were a recurrent disease to which African states are liable.

Such phrases as "a relapse into tribalism" are apt to be used for any violent outbreak of local feeling although these are caused as often by new politico-economic rivalries as by traditional ones. These new

33

ethnic rivalries must now be discussed. It is my thesis that the coming of independence has created or aggravated intergroup tensions and conflicts which were not as significant before, ironical though this may sound.

First, the withdrawal of strongly centralized colonial governments led to attempts in some areas to settle intertribal grudges dating sometimes from the nineteenth century. The massacre of the Tutsi by their Hima serfs which followed the granting of independence to Ruanda, then a Belgian mandated territory, is a case in point. The resentment of many Congolese people to the Luba and Kongo tribes who were formerly dominant in the area has also been held responsible, at least in part, for the destruction and murder which decimated the Belgian Congo once it had attained independent rule. On the whole, grievances based on unhappy historical incidents do not seem to have been as important a basis for hostilities as new rivalries between traditional ethnic groups or combinations of such groups. Competition for power in the central government is one such rivalry. Figure 1 (p. 21) shows that the governorship of each colonial territory and all the senior official posts in the central government were filled by expatriate officials. Who was to be chosen as the figurehead in the East African territories once the British governor was gone? Kenya had its anticolonial hero, Jomo Kenyatta, a Kikuyu, but Uganda was torn by controversy over the presidency of its new state. Was it to be Mutesa II, the king of the powerful Ganda, or Milton Obote, the Prime Minister, a member of the Lango tribe? Who were to be the ministers, the senior civil servants, the army and police heads?

These key posts still paid the inflated salaries thought necessary to attract able expatriates, as many writers on decolonization have pointed out. Arthur Lewis estimated these salaries to be four or five times as high as the income of the average peasant in West Africa.[2] For ex-French territories, René Dumont makes similar comparisons between the pay of senior African officials and deputies and the man-in-the-bush. A deputy in a French-speaking territory earns as much in one and a half months, he suggests, as a peasant in thirty-six years.[3] No wonder such posts were and are highly coveted, and members of different ethnic groups compete for them. The problem is not a new one. Differential access to the top ranks in the civil service is always a source of contention in multicultural states—whether in the Italian Tyrol, where Austrians feel deprived of their former rights to positions in the local government service, or in South Africa, where British and Afrikaners competed at one time for such posts. Those who analyze the mounting tension in the new African states now find it necessary to study not only the ethnic composition of their national assemblies but also that of their ministries, their armies, and their police. For instance, during a recent coup in Nigeria (January 1966), some events were explained by the fact that the officers of the Nigerian army were Ibo from the south-eastern region, while the rank-and-file had been recruited from the northern region; and the course of the disturbances in Uganda in May of the same year seems to have been affected by the fact that both the army and police came from the northern tribes. The officers also came from these areas; none were from the dominant Ganda to the south.

Second, economic rivalry between regions seems to

2 W. Arthur Lewis, *Politics in West Africa* (London: Allen and Unwin, 1965), p. 31.
3 René Dumont, *False Start in Africa,* trans. Phyllis Nauts Ott (London: André Deutsch, 1966), p. 81.

have increased since the establishment of independent rule. Of course, environmental inequalities between the different districts existed long before the period of colonial government. Lewis estimates that the per capita income of West Africans living in the belt with an average yearly rainfall of seventy inches is five times as high as that of the people who live in a belt with an average annual rainfall of thirty inches.[4] The arrival of European administrators and traders at the end of the nineteenth century often increased these environmental differentials. The placing of a railway or the building of a town gave almost immediate opportunities for advance to the people of the selected area. The choice of Nairobi as the site for a European town brought economic advantages to the Kikuyu in whose country the town was built, as well as depriving them of considerable stretches of their land. The Kikuyu became known as the best-educated people in Kenya. They found employment all over the territory and tended to become objects of jealousy and resentment. The Luo of Nyanza province, Kenya, formed another group of adaptable, ambitious traders, clerks, and artisans who also proved more successful than members of other tribes. When political parties formed in Kenya in 1960, it was the Kenya African Democratic Union (KADU), a union of the lesser tribes, which opposed the Kenya African National Union (KANU), the party of the Kikuyu and Luo, the group which finally formed the government. In the same way, the building of Elizabethville in the traditional territory of the Luba gave these people new economic opportunities. They became the technicians, drivers, and traders of the southern Congo and also prospered as cash-croppers. Their success also was resented by the other

[4] Lewis, p. 23.

ethnic groups in the region. Uganda furnishes another example of the same phenomenon.

In other words, the achievement of independence found some tribal groups which had "taken off" (in the Rostow sense) and some which had not. This is the problem of the economists' "advanced enclaves": rivalry between the tribal "haves" and "have-nots," and often a fierce determination of the "haves" to maintain the advantages fortune has given them and not to share them with their less advanced fellows. In Uganda, the difference between the standard of living of the wealthy Ganda and that of the naked Karomojong herdsmen on the eastern border was so great that the anxieties of the richer tribe, which saw itself being pulled down to the level of the poorer, were understandable if not admirable.

Lewis stresses the political effects of regional inequalities. He claims, in fact, that "tribal differences might disappear easily in the modern world if all tribes were equal economically" and he considers that advanced regions should not have to support the backward.[5] The latter view obviously is highly controversial but it certainly highlights the problem of ethnic rivalries and separatist tendencies based on new economic developments rather than on traditional attitudes.

Finally, the introduction of universal suffrage for which the African élite and their European supporters fought for so long has also intensified intergroup rivalry in a way not anticipated at the time. African political parties have often been regionally and even tribally based. In Kenya, for example, the KANU party was mainly a Kikuyu and Luo party. In the Congo, the Luba formed the backbone of *L'Association des Baluba du*

[5] *Ibid.*, pp. 23, 51.

Katanga (BALUBAKAT), associated with the name of Albert Kalonji. The party called *Confédération des Associations du Katanga* (CONAKAT) was under Lunda leadership and associated with the name of Moise Tshombe, while the Kongo of Leopoldville dominated *L'Alliance des Bakongo* (ABAKO), the party of Joseph Kasavubu. The old African Liberal Movement of Ghana was Ashanti-based. In Nigeria, the National Council for Nigeria and the Cameroons (NCNC) was an Ibo movement; the Action Group was dominated by the Yoruba; the Northern Peoples' Congress (NPC) was a northern territories group as the name implies. The long struggle to form a national party in Uganda, described below, was a result of the dominance of one ethnic group.

The introduction of universal franchise, then, intended among other things to liberate Africans from their tribal allegiances, sometimes strengthened old ethnic rivalries. In some territories, the system even seems to have created a sense of tribal identity which did not exist before. Daniel Biebuyck suggests that the Mongo people, who consisted originally of a collection of small independent communities widely scattered over the Congo region and without a sense of tribal identity, were organized into a single political party by Patrice Lumumba, a member of this ethnic group, and formed the basis of his national party, the *Mouvement National Congolais* (MNC). Just because they were so widely distributed in five out of the six provinces in which they were found in considerable numbers, they were able to return a member of the MNC to the Chamber of Deputies.[6] This would not have been possible if the Mongo

[6] Daniel Biebuyck and Mary Douglas, *Congo Tribes and Parties*, RAI Pamphlet, No. 1 (London: Royal Anthropological Institute, 1961), pp. 24-25.

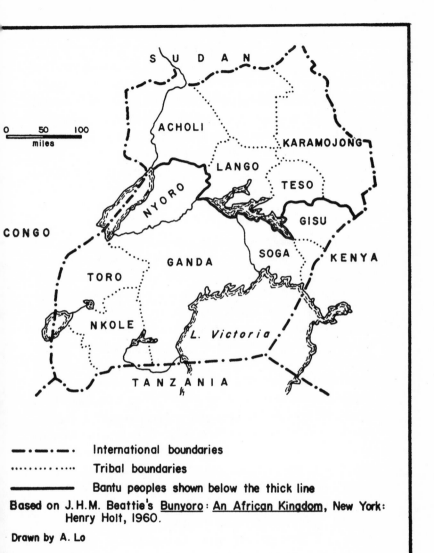

—··—··—	International boundaries
·············	Tribal boundaries
———————	Bantu peoples shown below the thick line

Based on J.H.M. Beattie's <u>Bunyoro</u>: <u>An African Kingdom</u>, New York: Henry Holt, 1960.

Drawn by A. Lo

TRIBAL MAP OF UGANDA

had all been included in a single province, as was common in the case of a large tribe like the Luba or Kongo which had built up an empire in the old days. The Mongo became conscious of their political power apparently through taking part in the election; yet it would hardly be possible to describe their new feeling of identity as a "reversion to tribalism." European observers have shown too little understanding of the many economic and political factors contributing to regional and tribal rivalry.

THE SPECIAL CASE OF UGANDA

In 1958, four years before independence, Uganda was reckoned to have a population of about six million people, divided into twenty sizeable ethnic groups. These peoples are sharply demarcated into three main cultural divisions: the Bantu, the Nilotic, and the Nilo-Hamitic (see the tribal map of Uganda). Within the Bantu-speaking peoples are the four kingdoms of Buganda, Bunyoro, Toro, and Ankole to the south and west of Uganda, and the multiple chiefdoms which formed Busoga on the eastern border of Buganda. This group of peoples, known as the Interlacustrine Bantu, speak similar dialects and tend to use the same school textbooks. They have many cultural features in common, particularly their attitude to authority, their hierarchy of chiefs and kings, and their form of spirit worship. Buganda and Toro signed agreements with the British Protectorate government in 1900, Ankole in 1901, and Bunyoro in 1933. These treaties recognized the kings and governments of these polities; hence, the four kingdoms are often referred to as the Treaty States. The other Bantu tribes in the territory are acephalous and organized in segmenting clans and lineages. The most important are the Gisu on the slopes and foothills of Mount Elgon, and the Kiga to the west of Uganda on its border with Ruanda and the Congo.

The non-Bantu peoples of this territory include the Nilotic-speaking peoples living in the less fertile grasslands to the north of Uganda—the Acholi, Alur, and Lugbara—as well as the tribes reckoned as Nilo-Hamites —the Lango, the Teso, and the nomadic herdsmen on the Kenya border known as the Karomojong. The Acholi have formed the mainstay of the police and army of Uganda and figured prominently in the disturbances of 1965 and 1966. The Alur and Lugbara live mainly in a poor environment and migrate to wealthy Buganda to the south to find the money they need. The Teso and Lango took to cash crops about 1910 after cotton had been introduced in Buganda, and almost abandoned the pastoral activities which were previously their major source of livelihood. The Karomojong, on the other hand, rejected the civilization of Europe, as have the kindred Turkana and Suk over the Kenya border. They are the image of naked savagery for their disapproving Bantu neighbours to the south.

None of the Nilotic and Nilo-Hamitic peoples of Uganda had achieved a centralized government by the time of Speke's visit in 1862. They were organized on a clan and lineage basis with an added division into age-sets in the case of the Lango, Teso, and Karomojong. The eastern district inhabited by the Kumam, Teso, and Lango was administered by Semei Kakunguru, a Ganda chief, in 1896; and Ganda agents remained in control over the Teso until 1913. Thus a Ganda-type administration was introduced in these areas as well as in Kigezi on the western borders of Uganda (1911). Yet the political ideas of these segmentary people remained different

41

from those of the inhabitants of the Bantu kingdoms; they were considered backward by their southern neighbours.

BUGANDA: THE PROBLEMS OF AN ADVANCED ENCLAVE

Uganda exhibits, in an extreme form, the problem of the advanced enclave, and it is for this reason that this state is given a special examination. The people who were most advanced politically, economically, and educationally were the Ganda, the inhabitants of Buganda, the largest of the Treaty States. To begin with, the Ganda are nearly twice the size of any other ethnic group in Uganda. In the years preceding independence, they formed 17 per cent of the total population whereas the next largest tribes totalled respectively 9.4 per cent of the population (Teso), 8.7 per cent (Soga), and 5.9 per cent (Nyoro). The other ethnic groups were even smaller.

Buganda was also the most politically advanced of the interlacustrine kingdoms when Speke visited the region in 1862. He described the size of the king's capital;[7] the constant and abject homage paid to the monarch, the kabaka; the elaboration of the life of the court; its ministers and priests and executioners; and the network of roads radiating from the capital to the headquarters of the greater and lesser authorities in the different districts. We now know that the system was unusually centralized compared with the political organization of other African tribes. The ministers and administrative chiefs at the district and subdistrict levels were appointed directly by the kabaka, and were deprived of

[7] Apolo Kagwa estimated the size of the capital as ten thousand. *Ekitabo kye Mpisa za Baganda*, 1st ed., 1905 (Kampala: Uganda Society, 1952), pp. 292-97.

office if he so desired. By the middle and end of the nineteenth century, only two local hereditary chiefs had survived.[8] All other political appointments were in the
hands of the king and his chief minister, the *katikkiro*.
The kabaka was able to exact a regular tax collected by
his own tax-gatherers, as distinct from the sporadic tribute brought to the Bantu chiefs in other parts of East,
Central, and South Africa. Mutesa I, who ruled from
1856 to 1884, had a personal standing army at his capital
as well as the levies raised by each county chief on occa-
sion. He also had a "fleet" of 104 canoes on Lake Victoria
as well as control over 10,000 other canoes, according to
Apolo Kagwa. He thus controlled the Arab dhow trade.

The Ganda also had a tradition of superiority over
the surrounding peoples. Their kings exacted tribute
from the Soga and other peoples on their eastern border,
from A. A. Kooki on their western border, and occasion-
ally from the Nyoro. Writing in 1878, Stanley estimated
the size of Mutesa I's "empire" as 2.8 million, obviously
including people who paid tribute intermittently as well
as those who paid it on a more permanent basis.[9] In
1953, his great-grandson, Mutesa II, showed visitors a
map illustrating the extent of the territory which he felt
should belong to Buganda; it included a sizeable slice
of Kenya. The Ganda were inordinately proud of this
position of superiority. They valued their history, traced
back through thirty-four kabakas, who were still hon-
oured in royal shrines where drums and regalia were
kept. They boasted of their military exploits and the size
of their empire. Mutesa I thought he was the greatest
monarch in the world until Stanley told him about

[8] The Mugema in Busiro (the leader of the monkey clan) and the
Kamswaga of Kooki.
[9] Henry Morton Stanley, *Through the Dark Continent*, vol. 1 (New
York: Harpers, 1878), p. 401.

Queen Victoria. He is said to have then proposed marriage to her!

When the British began their administration of Uganda in 1890, the date of Lugard's arrival in the country, the predominance of Buganda over her neighbours was increased rather than diminished. Ganda forces united with the British to defeat the Nyoro in 1894, and as a result Buganda gained five counties from Bunyoro as her reward. In other parts of Uganda, Ganda agents administered the territories inhabited by other tribes. Kakunguru, the Ganda chief mentioned above, was given rule over Bugerere, now a county of Buganda, after the 1893-94 war with Bunyoro. From 1896 to 1902, he was given charge of the pacification of the Lango and Kumam in the Lake Kyoga area; afterwards Ganda agents were used there. From 1899 to 1904, he was also engaged in administering the Teso, while Ganda agents were left in charge of this area until 1913. Kakunguru was then made president of a new council, designed to unify the chiefdoms of Busoga, from 1908 to 1913. In 1911, the boundaries of what is now known as Kigezi, on the Ruanda border, were fixed, and Ganda agents were appointed there.[10] In each case, the Ganda system of county, subcounty, and "parish" chiefs was introduced with councils at each level, and Luganda was used as the language of administration and even the medium of instruction in the schools. No wonder the Ganda were confirmed in their belief of their superiority over the other peoples of Uganda.

By the Uganda Agreement signed with the Protectorate government in 1900, the Ganda kabaka and their traditional system of government were officially recog-

[10] Kenneth Ingham, *The Making of Modern Uganda* (London: Allen and Unwin, 1958), pp. 76, 117-18, 122.

nized. Nevertheless, they showed themselves eager to adopt many British administrative practices. The Christian chiefs in power at the end of the nineteenth century were deeply committed to westernization and to European ideas of progress.[11] Their central council, the *Great Lukiiko,* originally a set of notables gathered to pay homage to the king, under British guidance became a Buganda parliament with its own sphere of local legislation.[12] The Ganda became intensely proud of it and many believed it to be a traditional institution. Their pride in the proliferation of committees in their central government, its filing system, records, and minute-keeping, was as great as that they felt for their monarchy, its royal pomp and sacred drums. In fact, L. A. Fallers has pointed out that "many western ideas of government, Anglican and Roman Catholic Christianity, the motivations appropriate to a money economy"[13] came to be considered part of Ganda culture and something which the other peoples of Uganda were without. Wealthy Ganda lived as much as possible like Europeans of the period, and in 1950, they referred to members of other tribes as "natives," classing themselves as "Europeans."

In the educational field, the Ganda were the most advanced people in Uganda. This was mainly because both the Catholic and Protestant missionaries who arrived in 1870 were forbidden to leave the Kampala area where Mutesa I's capital was situated, and so Buganda got an educational head-start. The first secondary

11 See D. A. Low in D. A. Low and R. C. Pratt, *Buganda and British Overrule* (London: Oxford University Press, 1960), pp. 5-11; C. C. Wrigley, "The Changing Economic Structure of Buganda," in *The King's Men,* ed. L. A. Fallers (London: Oxford University Press, 1964), p. 26.

12 Though its members were officials and nominated men for many years, and the majority were not elected until 1953.

13 Fallers, *The King's Men,* p. 9.

45

schools were set up in this region; Buganda had the highest rate of secondary school and university educated citizens in Uganda in the years before independence. It is still the educational center of Uganda.

Uganda also was highly favoured economically. It lay in the fertile lake basin with an ample rainfall of forty inches, which made possible permanent settlement with plantain as the staple crop. It was an area highly suitable for the production of cotton, introduced in 1904. In fact, the bulk of Uganda's cotton was grown there until 1910 when its cultivation spread to other areas. Later, after World War II, cotton began to yield to robusta coffee; this high-income crop attracted the more commercially minded farmers who recognized that it was a time of unprecedented prices for primary products like coffee. The railway was extended from Jinja to Kampala in 1931; and Kampala, the seat of the kabaka's government, then became the industrial and commercial centre of Uganda even though the Protectorate government was sited at Entebbe, 24 miles away but still in Buganda. Immigrants from poorer parts of Uganda and from Ruanda, Urundi, and Kenya poured into the country to work on Ganda farms or to settle in the countryside and man the new industries.

In fact it would be difficult to find a more strikng instance of an ethnic group in an African state so relatively advanced in the political, educational, and economic fields and which could most aptly be described as an advanced enclave. The Ganda were the pivotal tribe in Uganda. In Fallers' words, they "contributed a powerful impulse towards modernization but have also remained intensely chauvinistic" and proud of their own history and culture.[14]

14 *Ibid.*, p. 11.

46

With the promise of independence for Uganda, it was assumed that here, as elsewhere in Africa, the intelligentsia of Uganda would lead the fight for freedom; and the intelligentsia were mainly in Buganda. Yet, when Sir Andrew Cohen was appointed governor in 1952 and came to the country determined to hasten the introduction of self-government, troubles became apparent.

Buganda had fought for many years against inclusion in wider political units in which she felt she would lose her identity. In 1921, the Kabaka and his Prime Minister wrote to protest against the setting up of a legislative council in Uganda, fearing that "the interests and welfare of the Buganda will be relegated to the background and will necessarily form a secondary consideration in the deliberations of the Council in view of the general interests and progress of the whole Protectorate."[15] "Buganda first and Buganda alone" was the motto. In 1924, the *Great Lukiiko* protested against the recommendations of the Commission on Closer Union in East Africa, and in 1950 against the setting up of common East African High Commission services. In 1953, at a Nairobi luncheon, it was the Secretary of State's reference to the possibility of a federation of East African states which so agitated the Ganda *Lukiiko* as to cause a head-on collision between the Protectorate and the Buganda governments, and which resulted in the deportation of the Kabaka to England. Buganda was stunned at this event. Women wept in the streets. All festivities were put to an end. The royal drums were silenced. Dancing was stopped. The inter-clan football matches were given up. The Ganda did not riot, but they went on strike for nearly a year, refusing to pay taxes and sometimes refusing

[15] Cited in David Apter, *The Political Kingdom in Uganda* (Princeton: Princeton University Press, 1961), p. 166.

to meet European officials. Most interesting of all perhaps was the fact that the educated members of this comparatively well-educated people sided with the traditionalists on the issue, though before they often had been critical of the Kabaka. The monarchy stood for Buganda as a political entity and for the superiority of Buganda over other people. Therefore, boys and girls from secondary schools and university graduates returned to the traditional ways when the kingship was attacked (see above, p. 13). The whole phenomenon illustrated in striking fashion the use of customs and clothing, regarded as symbolic of a past way of life, by a people which felt its identity threatened. A reversion to tribalism? In one sense, perhaps, but the people continued the economic practices of the western world of which they were now part. They paid and accepted wages, used banks, started trading and industrial enterprises, and newspapers; much of the western machinery of administration they had adopted continued to function, in however inefficient a way.

It became clear during the Kabaka's absence that Uganda could not function without the participation of its richest and most important ethnic group, unless the kingdom of Buganda were destroyed by force. The Protectorate government did not want to use force and therefore it had to compromise with the Ganda, a process so difficult that it took nearly eight years. The Kabaka was returned in 1954 with a new constitution for Buganda framed by the Hancock Committee and a promise that the *Lukiiko* would appoint representatives to the Legislative Assembly—a promise that was not kept. The framing of a constitution for Uganda as a whole was much more difficult. It was only achieved after three commissions had sat: the Wilde Commission

48

of 1959, the Munster Commission of 1961, and the Molson Commission of 1962. A difficult compromise was reached three months before the date of independence (October 1962).

The problems were clear. How was Buganda to be persuaded to accept a position as a mere province in a unitary Uganda? Was it possible to adjust the relative positions of the King of Buganda to that of the future President of Uganda and the Prime Minister of the whole country? The Ganda had always been ready to accept a unitary Uganda with Buganda at its head, but not willing to be reduced to the equal of the other tribal groups in Uganda. As one of her spokesmen said, "We are a nation, not a tribe like the Welsh." What was to be the position of the capital of Uganda situated in the heart of the Buganda kingdom? What financial arrangements were to be made between this wealthy province and the poorer parts of Uganda? Who would control the army and the police? Lastly, an issue which recently had become important, how would Buganda be persuaded to give up the "lost counties," the parts of Bunyoro she had been given by Lugard after the war of 1883 and which Bunyoro now reclaimed?

During the protracted negotiations on these points, the *Lukiiko* of Buganda fought every inch of the way. The Ganda refused to take part in the general elections in 1958, started a trade blockade in 1959, and their *Lukiiko* solemnly declared the British Protectorate to be at an end "in the name of God and the Nation" in January 1961. Buganda boycotted elections in that year, but subsequently attended the Munster Conference in London, and there attained something like the position it wanted as a "single Federal Kingdom in a composite state"; it achieved favourable compromises concerning

49

the police, the high court, and the control of Kampala; and it also received more than its share of the funds. There was to be a special commission on the "lost counties."

There remained the general election planned for April 1962. Universal franchise in these circumstances of course was fraught with difficulties, as Lewis pointed out in the case of the West African states.[16] Uganda was slow to develop a national radical party. Her most educated citizens were Ganda and these were the men who initiated the first political parties. The numerous vernacular newspapers which appeared during the 1950s were written in Luganda and were edited mainly by Ganda. But Ganda-led parties tended to break down when the integrity of Buganda was threatened. Thus the Uganda National Congress, founded in 1952 as a party of all races and tribes, supported the Kabaka after his deportation in 1953 and united with traditionalist Ganda groups to agitate for their king's return. It then divided into many splinter groups. The Democratic party, a mainly Catholic group, was also a national organization (there were of course Catholics distributed throughout Uganda). The Democrats won the 1961 election which most of the people of Buganda boycotted, but they failed to win the loyalty of the Ganda. Obote, the present Prime Minister, a Lango, started his own national party, the Uganda People's Congress (UPC) in Lango in 1957-58. In 1962, he had the political acumen to offer alliance to a new Ganda traditionalist party, the Kabaka Yekka (KY), that is, "Kabaka only," which had been formed in 1961. This curious alliance between a national radical party and a Ganda royalist party was able to oust the Democrats in the election of

16 Lewis, Chapter 2.

April 1962. It was this step which made possible independence for Uganda in October 1962, with the winning coalition securing 67 votes in the National Assembly, the UPC 43, the KY 24, and the Democrats 24.

During the independence celebrations, the coming struggle for power between Obote, the Prime Minister, and Mutesa II, King of the largely autonomous "Federal State" of Buganda, was only barely concealed. Obote's party, the UPC, produced posters showing a large figure of the Prime Minister on a map of Uganda and a tiny figure of the Kabaka in Buganda, while the KY poster had Mutesa II's figure resplendent in the centre with Obote as a very small and shadowy form on the periphery. The Kabaka was appointed President, a post intended as a constitutional figurehead, when the British Governor left, but this did not end the power struggle. Obote, a great admirer of Kwame Nkrumah, was anxious to build up a national state of Uganda. The Kabaka and his *Lukiiko*, who were struggling for the autonomy of Buganda, also began to aim at the building up of a southern Bantu state composed of the four kingdoms and Busoga in opposition to the northern peoples.

Obote survived Buganda's hostility to a referendum on the "lost counties," which recommended the return of the territory to Bunyoro (1964) and which incidentally won him support in that district. But on 14 February 1966 he was challenged by the Secretary-General of the KY and some members of his own party, and accused of corruption. Events then moved rapidy. On 22 February he took full power of government and imprisoned five ministers, all from the southern region. He suspended the constitution (24 February), assumed the President's power, and locked the Kabaka out of his official residence (6 March). On 15 April he introduced a new constitution accepted, apparently unread, by a show of hands. This gave him executive powers as President, and virtually brought to an end Buganda's federal position. The *Lukiiko* was powerless. It challenged the legality of the constitutional changes on 13 March, and on 24 May was ill-advised enough to issue an ultimatum to the central government, telling it to remove itself from the soil of Buganda by 30 May. Obote ordered an attack on the Kabaka's palace on 25 May. The Kabaka's guard fought back and over a thousand soldiers and civilians were reported killed. The king escaped to England; the palace was in smoke; the royal drums and other regalia were wantonly destroyed. Subsequent disturbances in the countryside were put down, apparently with great brutality, by police almost entirely recruited from the north. Another one-party state was born.

Since this writing, the destruction of the kingdoms of Uganda has gone further. By the new Uganda Constitution of 16 June 1967, Uganda was declared a Republic without constituent kingdoms. The Kabaka is still in England. The other kings are pensioned off. The regalia and drums of each of these monarchs are either destroyed or else housed in the Kampala museum. Buganda has been divided into four districts and, administratively speaking, no longer exists as a unit.

This is one end to the problem of the advanced enclave and one similar to the solution reached by Nkrumah in the case of the Ashanti in Ghana. Could so much bloodshed and bitterness have been avoided if the Protectorate government had been less opposed to federal constitutions in the years before 1962, and had accepted the idea of more semi-autonomous states, for instance, in the south? Would a different system of election weighted to represent regional interests have helped, as

Lewis suggests? Would a quicker and more stable solution have been reached if the colonial government had used a display of force when the Kabaka was deported and had cut Buganda down to size—however much it would have meant reversing its previous policy?

More important perhaps is the question of the survival of Ganda values. Will they recover quickly from what is described as sullen resentment, or will the people divide themselves for a time into two sections—an ambitious political élite struggling for positions in the central government, and a tradition-oriented peasant population still longing for Buganda's past glory? Will Obote be able to find enough efficient administrators from the north to take charge of the new type of local administration? A strict press censorship so far has prevented observers from answering these questions.

CHAPTER III:
RURAL DEVELOPMENT IN A
MULTICULTURAL STATE

I TURN now to the problems of development, and hence of administration, at the village and neighbourhood level, the base of the structural pyramid shown in Figure 1, (p. 21). This is the sphere of life in which traditional systems of administration and agricultural practice are most firmly entrenched, but it is also the level at which the next agricultural revolution must take place, if it is to take place at all. One such revolution of course has occurred. It was produced by the introduction of cash crops, most of them new to the areas concerned, and by the building of railways and highroads which made it possible to export these commodities. In East Africa, this revolution in peasant production took place between 1900 and the beginning of World War II. The development was patchy but, in favourable areas, dramatic. This was especially the case in Uganda where agricultural production remained almost entirely in African hands after attempts at European plantation economy were abandoned early in the century. The railway from Mombasa to Nairobi was extended to Kisumu on Lake Victoria in 1902 and to Jinja in 1905. Cotton was introduced in South Uganda in 1904, and thereafter, as Table 2 shows, its production rose dramatically.[1]

[1] Harold B. Thomas and Robert Scott, *Uganda* (London: Oxford University Press, 1935), p. 505.

54

TABLE 2

COTTON PRODUCTION

Year	No. of 400 lb. bales exported	Value (£)
1905/6	241	1,089
1910/11	13,378	165,412
1920/21	47,695	3,778,931
1925/26	195,038	4,685,992

The production of coffee, which now surpasses that of cotton in value, also increased rapidly when the Protectorate government decided to encourage this crop in 1923; Table 3 shows acreages planted with coffee.[2]

TABLE 3

COFFEE PLANTED IN UGANDA

Year	Acres
1922	1,000
1925	1,787
1931	20,900
1934	30,349

The high prices of cotton and coffee in the postwar years led to a further increase in prosperity, especially for Buganda. In Tanzania, it was some time before the coast was linked to the hinterland, and the railway coverage in this vast territory was and is inadequate. A central railway from Dar-es-Salaam to Kigoma on Lake Victoria was completed in 1914 with branch lines from Tabora to Mwanza and Manyoni to Arusha in 1928 and 1933 respectively. A northern line from Tanga to Moshi in the coffee-producing area was finished in 1911 and was extended to Arusha in 1929.[3] But in Tanzania and Kenya,

2 Cited in C. C. Wrigley, *Crops and Wealth in Uganda*, East Africa Studies No. 12 (Kampala: East African Institute of Social Research, 1959), p. 42.
3 Lord Hailey, *An African Survey*, rev. ed. (London: Oxford University Press, 1957), pp. 1581-84.

production of cash crops by Africans lagged behind that of the European settlers with large plantations or estates; in the case of some crops, for instance coffee in Kenya, African cultivation was limited for some years in the interests of the white farmers. Nevertheless, when cotton was introduced in Tanzania—mainly in the Victoria basin in the 1930s—there was the same type of rapid advance as there had been in Uganda at the beginning of the century, while cotton production in the Nyanza province of Kenya showed a similar expansion, as Table 4 shows.[4]

TABLE 4

COTTON BALES EXPORTED

Tanzania		Kenya	
1931	*1936*	*1930*	*1935*
13,587	63,130	783	16,165

Coffee also proved a most suitable crop for the Bukoba and Kilimanjaro areas of Tanzania and for the highlands of Kenya. Production increased rapidly among the African farmers of these districts.

It is true that these success stories concern especially favoured areas and not the whole population. It is also true that the colonial administrators and agricultural officers of the time seem, in the light of recent experience, to have been unduly timid in their ideas of crops suited for peasant production. For instance, in Uganda, tea was thought to require expert European or Asian management as late as the 1950s, although it is now being grown successfully in the Kericho area of Kenya and in Uganda. Yet in spite of these tendencies a revolution had certainly begun.

[4] Lord Hailey, *An African Survey* (London: Oxford University Press, 1938), pp. 903, 909.

The second African revolution is still in process and dates from the years immediately following World War II. The concept of planned development for whole territories then became current; and African colonies, as they then were, began to frame five- or ten-year development programmes under expert advice for the first time. This second revolution was probably more difficult to effect than the first. It involved the extension of land under cultivation, and it was an era of hopes and disappointments for the widespread use of mechanical aids to cultivation. Machines in agriculture seemed to promise so much and often gave so little, mostly because of difficult terrain, high costs, or the peasants' inability to finance or maintain tractors.

But the second revolution also involved the better use of land already under cultivation. This meant not only the introduction of better strains of crops but also drastic changes in traditional ways of life, such as alterations in the system of land tenure to provide more efficient units of cultivation, and changes in rural leadership or in the cycle of agricultural activities to which the peasants were accustomed. For instance, experiment has shown that even an alteration in the traditional date of sowing may produce substantially higher yields in some areas with some crops. Dumont claims that in the Lake Chad area, changing the date of planting cotton from 1 July to 14 July gave thirty to sixty thousand more tons per annum.[5] In Uganda, it was reckoned that the planting of cotton in mid-June to mid-July instead of from August to September also considerably increased the yield per acre.[6]

[5] René Dumont, *False Start in Africa*, trans. Phyllis Nauts Ott (London: André Deutsch, 1966), p. 154.

[6] Uganda, Agricultural Department, *Record of Investigations*, No. 1 (J. H. Jameson) (Entebbe: Government Printer, 1950), p. 3.

Such changes in accepted patterns of land rights or traditional rules of agriculture may seem simple to the technical expert concerned with a single aspect of the problem, such as land registration or cotton production. But they may appear very difficult to the peasant involved, since changes in land tenure and in cultivation may mean alterations in social relationships, between a son and a father for instance, or changes in social grouping, perhaps in the homestead or the village. Even the altered dates of sowing and planting may necessitate quite drastic changes in the series of different activities of which the peasant's seasonal calendar is composed. It is here, in fact, that anthropological knowledge of economic systems and economic attitudes could be of special help to the agricultural economist if this cooperation could be arranged.

Yet however difficult it may be for African peasants to visualize changes in their village and family structure and their economic activities, a second agricultural revolution evidently has to take place. We are constantly told that African states must depend first and foremost on primary production if they are to advance. It is estimated that in 1959, 96 per cent of the Africans in Uganda were in agriculture.[7] The figures show, too, that in Uganda 90 per cent of all export incomes are derived from agriculture; while in Tanzania, and also in Kenya, 80 per cent of the value of all exports and livestock came from the same source.[8] Evidently, East Africa still depends mainly on agriculture. For this reason, the present low level of production in many parts of the continent

[7] See Ralph Clark, "Programmes and Policies," in *Aid in Uganda* Part II (London: Overseas Development Institute, 1966), p. 17.

[8] K. G. V. Krishna, "Resources and Problems of Economic Development," in *The Transformation of East Africa*, ed. S. Diamond and F. G. Burke (New York: Basic Books, 1966), p. 548.

has to be raised dramatically, if the increasing population recorded in the recent censuses is to be fed, if the general standard of living is to be raised according to the expectations engendered among the people by the coming of independence, and—a point often forgotten—if a proper supply of food for the growing populations of East African towns is to be insured.

It is difficult to compare the relative productivity of agriculture in Europe and in peasant Africa in any meaningful way, but surprising figures sometimes appear. For instance, Table 5 is a calculation of the yields per man-hour for cereals and legumes in the United Kingdom, China, and Malawi, respectively.[9] Similar figures could no doubt be produced from other parts of Africa.

TABLE 5

YIELDS FOR CEREALS AND LEGUMES

Crop		Protein in lbs.	
		Per man-hour	Per acre
Cereals			
Wheat	(U.K.)	4.20	144.0
Maize	(China)	.51	94.5
Maize	(Malawi)	.37	74.2
Legumes			
Peas	(U.K.)	5.90	260.0
Groundnuts	(China)	.36	132.0
Groundnuts	(Malawi)	.17	83.0

Revolutions in peasant agriculture have been achieved in Africa by the opening of new markets and new systems of transport which I have described here as the first revolution, for example, the success of peasant cultivation of cotton and coffee in East Africa. Africans have

[9] Arthur Leslie Banks, ed., *The Development of Tropical and Sub-Tropical Countries* (London: Edward Arnold, 1954), p. 113.

59

generally taken advantage of such opportunities although not always the maximum advantage and not always with a quite spontaneous reaction. The first introduction of a crop has often required vigorous government propaganda and a measure of compulsion, whether the pressure has been applied by European or African authorities. Even Dumont, who writes with great disapproval of the use of penal sanctions in agriculture, speaks of "a transitory period of enlightened despotism."[10] Wrigley refers to such enlightened despotism in concrete terms when he quotes an elderly informant describing the first introduction of cotton into Uganda in 1904/5: "The chief beat the drum . . . and when we had gathered round he told us to dig the plots which had been marked out by the road-side and gave us cotton-seed to plant."[11] Where traditional authorities combined political and economic functions, as they did in most parts of Africa, new crops tended to be introduced in authoritarian fashion by the same ruler who gave orders in other spheres of life.

But after such initial pressure, the production of the new crop seems to have increased under its own impetus to a certain level, if not to the highest possible level. Compared to some of the more regimented types of cultivation described below, it certainly seems a laissez-faire system. It did not require the specialist's supervision and instruction which most new schemes inevitably involve.

The more directed methods of securing increased agricultural production during the period of colonial rule in Africa can be divided roughly under three headings: (1) schemes of forced cultivation, (2) government schemes for settlement, resettlement, or develop-

10 Dumont, *False Start,* p. 154.
11 Wrigley, *Crops and Wealth,* p. 16.

60

ment, and (3) an energetic improvement of the traditional methods of agriculture.

Forced cultivation was used by Belgian and French
authorities in order to raise revenue and to increase
the production of a new crop. It was assumed that forced
cultivation was also the quickest way of training African
peasants in the best agricultural methods. The Belgians
in fact used the term *cultivation educative* for this type
of forced production. Obligatory cultivation of cotton
was introduced by the Belgian government in cooperation with various commercial companies, and later
mainly with one company, the Compagnie Colonnière
Congolaise, in the Belgian Congo in 1917. By 1950,
about seventy thousand African peasants were employed
on this scheme. The French authorities in Equatorial
Africa introduced the same system, also in cooperation
with commercial companies, in 1924; by 1950, 40 per
cent of the total exports of the colony came from this
source.[12] Cotton cultivation was enforced by legal penalties. Dumont states that peasants in the Belgian Congo
were sentenced to eight days in prison for non-clearance
of land; thirteen days if the crops were not harvested in
time; and thirty days if the land was not correctly
burnt.[13]

It is clear that forced cultivation succeeded in one of
its aims, that is to say, the increase in the colonies' output. But it is difficult to be certain how far the educative
aim was realized in the sense that the peasant families
continued the agricultural practice they had learned
after the element of force had been removed.

It must be remembered that all farmers in the modern
world are subject to some regulations and some penalties
in the interest of the industry. The Ganda farmer fined

12 Hailey (1957), pp. 840-41.
13 Dumont, *False Start,* p. 70.

for not burning his cotton stalks by a certain month of the year may complain that he is acting under compulsion. But the term "forced cultivation" is used here to describe the obligatory planting of a crop rather than the enforcing of safety regulations of this kind. It raises the whole question of the use of force in promoting an agricultural revolution, and the personnel which is to apply this force, in a multicultural society in which local agricultural practices differ widely. Those charged with introducing new methods may be ignorant of these variations or unsympathetic to them.

At what stages of the proposed revolution is it efficient, in the economic sense, to use force? Should it be kept for preparatory processes such as initial clearance of the ground or the making of roads or should it be applied continuously from year to year? Should regulations be enforced by specialists from outside the culture or by members of the ethnic group concerned? These are questions which young African governments in a hurry will have to consider very carefully indeed.

Special schemes of settlement and development were based on the assumption that it is impossible to raise the standard of living of a whole population, but that special areas or special communities can be selected for intensive development, whether for experimental or for demonstration purposes. Schemes carried out by Protectorate and colonial governments in Africa included: (1) the development of new areas, (2) village improvement schemes, and (3) improved traditional methods.

The Gezira scheme for peasant cultivation of newly irrigated land in the south Sudan is probably the most famous experiment in the development of new areas. Irrigation, management, marketing, and research were provided jointly by the government and a commercial company. One million acres were prepared for cultivation in 1925, and by 1955, nearly 29,000 peasants were settled on measured forty-acre holdings (ten for cotton, ten for subsistence, and twenty for fallow). They received all the services offered in return for observing the agricultural regulations laid down. The management was expert and there was a "high degree of regimentation," but, as a result, the peasant per capita income rose from an average of £20 per annum before the last war to £200 in 1949 and £800 in 1951.[14]

The Swynnerton plan for the settlement of Africans in various parts of Kenya was also an ambitious scheme, born of the need to resettle Africans after the Mau Mau disturbances.[15] Its major recommendations were for the consolidation of African land holdings all over Kenya, on the basis of twelve special district surveys. The ultimate aim was to provide 600,000 African economic units of about ten acres, each producing an annual income of £100 or more. The Tana river irrigation schemes made it possible to put 5,000 acres under rice at Mwea Tebera and to settle 1,250 formerly landless tenants, with such success that it is planned to extend the acreage to 14,000 acres and to settle a total of 3,000 families.[16] Like the Gezira scheme, it was highly capitalized with expenditure on irrigation, soil reconditioning, and forestry control, besides road construction and conducting surveys. The settlements were under expatriate management and the farmers pledged to keep the regulations for

[14] Hailey (1957), pp. 1011-12.

[15] R. T. M. Swynnerton, *A Plan to Intensify the Development of African Agriculture in Kenya* (Nairobi: Government Printer, 1954), pp. 7-16.

[16] International Bank for Reconstruction and Development (IBRD), *The Economic Development of Kenya* (Baltimore: Johns Hopkins Press, 1963), pp. 77-78.

better agriculture required of them. The whole subject of settlement in Kenya has of course acquired additional importance since Swynnerton framed his ten-year plan (1954-64), because since independence, land formerly reserved for Europeans in the highland area has become available.

The most famous special development area in Tanzania in its Mandate and Trust days was probably the abortive groundnut scheme financed by the British Overseas Food Corporation in East Tanzania in 1946. Though a costly failure at the time, the land has been used for other forms of settlement, such as the African tenant scheme at Nachingwea, where selected Africans practised mechanized farming under supervision, the Urambo scheme, and others.[17]

All these large-scale settlement schemes were costly, depended on expatriate staff, and involved the creation of new communities formed of individuals and their families, rather than tribal groups. They were supervised by agricultural or other technical experts rather than by traditional administrative or political leaders.

Other schemes to help special groups in the community have concentrated on giving opportunities to enterprising individuals; they are not concerned with the formation of communities at all. The "improved farmers" scheme of Northern Rhodesia, introduced in 1947, by which farmers received a bonus per acre for reaching a special level of cultivation, is a case in point. As the result of this incentive, the income of one thousand farmers had doubled that of the ordinary peasant in 1952.[18] The "master farmer" scheme of the then South-

17 See International Bank for Reconstruction and Development (IBRD) *The Economic Development of Tanganyika* (Baltimore: Johns Hopkins Press, 1961), pp. 130-33.
18 Hailey (1957), pp. 848-49.

ern Rhodesia, and the "better farmers" singled out for special bonuses in the Nyanza province of Kenya, fall into the same category

Village improvement schemes differed from the former two categories in that they were planned to improve existing communities rather than to create new ones. The selected village was to provide for all sorts of experiments in better housing, sanitation, well-digging, and cooking methods, as well as in cultivation, irrigation, and road-making. Its influence was to spread to surrounding communities by what was later described as a "halo" effect, or the "spot" method of development. It was of course suited only to regions in which the people lived in sizeable villages and not in parts of Kenya or North Uganda where the settlement unit was little more than a homestead.

The model village approach depended, like the new settlement schemes, on outside leadership and, during the colonial period, on expatriate leadership. It depended too on the vigorous and enthusiastic district commissioner or agricultural officer who either organized the building of new roads, the opening of local markets, the planning of new houses and schools, and the teaching of new agricultural practices, or who persuaded the people to do these things themselves. An example is the famous Udi experiment in Nigeria.

The cost of such leadership was much less than that of the many technical experts needed for schemes of the Gezira type, because the leaders were single, "polivalent"[19] social welfare authorities in charge of all activities. But even so the expense of expatriate supervision

[19] To use a term fashionable in colonial welfare circles after World War II.

still prevented any very wide extension of these experiments, and there was still the problem, never finally solved, of assuring the continuity of effort once the external leadership had been removed. Village community developments became an essential part of the rural policy of the new independent government of Tanzania in its first years of office.

The last and most common method of introducing better agriculture was the improved traditional method. The first agricultural revolution was in fact carried out by traditional authorities, whether they were chiefs, clan-heads, or elders. These were the leaders accepted by the colonial authorities. Even in Kenya, which prides itself on never having been an indirect rule area, the lower level of authorities were traditional, or very like the traditional, even if the higher chiefs were civil servants appointed by the central government. These traditional heads, whether literate or not, enforced the minimal regulations for the protection of the land such as soil erosion measures; they supervised pest eradication, or the burning of crop stalks, and organized the distribution of new seeds.

Where there is a great gap in technical knowledge between one culture and another, and the government of the better-equipped culture is determined to pass on its expertise to the less well-equipped, then there must be an intermediary between one group and the other, between the dominant and the subject in colonial days or between the central authorities and the local ones after independence has been granted. The "native authorities" were these intermediaries. The first two levels of chief in Figure 1 (p. 21) were interpreters of the colonial government's regulations to the people; sometimes they also explained the peasant's views to the

66

government. Much has been written on the difficulties of chiefs and other traditional rulers in this facing-both-ways position. They were either praised by the colonial government as "progressive," and hated by their people as quislings; or they were criticized by the colonial authorities as being inefficient and backward, and admired by their own subjects.[20]

Below these were the third or fourth tier of authorities: the village headman, the minimal lineage heads, the heads of tiny districts, ridges, or valleys. These were the men engaged in direct face-to-face supervision, the men on the battered old bicycles, travelling slowly from homestead to homestead, perhaps the hardest worked and certainly the least rewarded of all the agents of change. In a society in which the majority of the people are illiterate, radio has poor coverage (radios are, in any case, too expensive for the majority of the peasants), and communications are poor, these low-level authorities have to be very numerous. In the Essex village where I live there were 213 adult inhabitants in 1965. We are expected to observe a number of laws or by-laws as to driving, the registration of births, education, agriculture, and the disposal of waste; but we do not require a headman to inform us of these, to exhort or to scold us. Most of the regulations are familiar rules and their observation does not mean great changes in our habits of living, as do many of the rules now imposed on African peasants. Education in welfare and agriculture and the inculcation of new standards of hygiene and nutrition would depend on the mass media in Great Britain, for

[20] Descriptive accounts of the situation are to be found in L. A. Fallers, *Bantu Bureaucracy* (Cambridge, England: W. Heffer, 1956), pp. 180-203 and A. I. Richards, ed., *East African Chiefs* (London: Faber & Faber, 1960), pp. 363-67.

example, and not on direct contact with a village head-man or a meeting of a village council. In the African village, these forms of publicity hardly exist; and the greater the changes contemplated, the greater the need for supervision and education personnel in the agricultural field. Traditional leaders at the village level, un-paid, or poorly paid, often working for traditional motives such as identification with the community or desire for prestige, carried out these functions, some-times efficiently and sometimes not, in colonial days.

During the second stage of rural betterment attempted before and after World War II, the native authorities were supplemented by trained technical instructors and agricultural assistants of all kinds. Some of the larger political units, such as the kingdom of Buganda, had many agricultural assistants, some centred at the head-quarters of the polity and some at the district or sub-district level. Buganda had its own Ministry of Natural Resources after 1954, and its own land registry office. Most of the richer native authorities also had their own capital equipment. Lorries labelled "Busoga Native Authority" or "Bukoba Native Authority" crashed 'round the countryside. Correspondence on agricultural matters was conducted on tribal writing paper, often with a symbol, such as a lion or an elephant, in place of, say, a maple leaf or the royal cipher. In Buganda, en-velopes were headed "On the service of His Highness the Kabaka" and replies came from across the road marked "On the service of Her Majesty the Queen."

Many different types of polity were used to implement rural measures, under the supervision of a colonial agricultural officer, of course. In South Uganda and North Tanzania, hereditary kings with ritual powers and a hierarchy of chiefs below them were first recognized,

68

and then given many new functions. In Arusha, the authority system was based on age-grades; among the Hehe, there was a council of clan-heads under a chief drawn from a royal clan, and in the coastal belt of Tanzania the Arab *liwali*, who functioned under German rule, remained.

Traditional councils survived and performed a special function in agricultural education, but they were made more democratic. In Tanzania with its many small tribal groups, the ingenuity displayed by the Trust authorities in amalgamating traditional and elected authorities was amazing. In the fifties, for instance, a federacy of chiefs in Sukumaland met with elected representatives. In Usambara, chiefs and sub-chiefs met with popularly chosen members; and in the Masai country a new type of area council was elected by the traditional age-grades and by kinship units, and these area councils sent representatives to a Masai Federal Council. The variety of institutional arrangements was therefore great, and, in spite of British efforts to amalgamate small units into larger, a great number still remained. Hailey records the existence of 386 native authorities, 800 native courts, and 51 treasuries in Tanzania in 1952.[21] No wonder the reforming political scientists and economists from Europe and America, who appeared in such numbers in East Africa during the sixties, were horrified by such a patchwork of institutional arrangements.

The use of traditional authorities as agents of agricultural revolution had many obvious disadvantages. The chiefs were not trained in modern agricultural science and many were uneducated in the modern sense.[22] They

[21] Hailey (1957), pp. 472-76.
[22] In 1950, 68 per cent of Ganda higher chiefs had secondary education; 54 per cent of Nyoro but no Alur higher chiefs and only 13 per cent of Zinza as quoted in Richards, p. 367.

had many other duties of an administrative kind. Yet, the use of these authorities had many advantages in the initial stages of rural betterment and some assets which more modern technical assistants have failed to achieve. Traditional leaders were accepted by their people, who expected to obey them in almost every aspect of life. Like the British district commissioners of old, they were multipurpose agents of welfare. In precolonial days chiefs combined many roles. They might be judges and rainmakers; senior clansmen and age-grade elders; military leaders and priests. In particular, they combined political and economic functions. Village headmen gave out land for cultivation, organized economic activities, kept order, and decided disputes. In colonial days, they had to add the duties of sanitary inspectors, agricultural and educational supervisors, rural engineers, and road foremen. In the 1940s, there was much discussion of the relative merits of expert help for African villages (in the form of separate agricultural and health inspectors or assistants), and the single polivalent or multipurpose welfare worker. The point was raised again by the mission to Tanzania organized by the International Bank for Reconstruction and Development in 1961,[23] and it will no doubt be a continuing controversy. The traditional authorities of colonial days were polivalent welfare workers, besides possibly being rain magicians or chiefs as well.

Chiefs, especially at the lower headman level, knew their people intimately. They saw them as kinship groups interconnected by marriages, age-old disputes, or land rights. This is the sort of familiarity on which leaders with no force to back them often had to rely. (This was expressed to me by a small Zambian chief

[23] IBRD, *Tanganyika*, pp. 110-12.

who said, "No, Madam! I have no diploma in administration but I know which villagers will come when I
want the work done!") The administration of a community by a member of that community is an entirely
different process from administration by an outside
authority, whether expatriate or not, as in the big
settlement schemes described above. It may well be less
efficient at a high level and more efficient at a village
level.

The old village councils were also essential parts of
the administration. Their meetings were educational in
the sense that they were the best available means of dis-
seminating information in a preliterate community.
Attendance was not limited in size; the men who came
represented groups, villages, or lineages, and what they
heard or said at the meeting was passed around these
particular groups. Anthropologists have found that the
council is also a means of committing villagers to action.
Men who took part in protracted discussions and agreed
in public with the decision reached thereby felt themselves committed to carrying out the proposed action.
This is a type of participant action which might well be
the envy of those who bewail the apathy of English
villagers toward their parish councils!

The lowest level of traditional authority, the headman
or the small lineage elder, often worked unpaid or was
poorly paid. This is a point which African governments
will have to consider when weighing the pros and cons
of rural development programmes.

This is not to maintain that these traditional local
leaders were always, or even often, efficient agents of
change. Many were old, conservative, and satisfied with
things as they were. They achieved the first agricultural
revolution, but at a pace much too slow to satisfy the

needs of today. Their leadership depended on traditional incentives and the working of a series of family
and kinship institutions of which they were themselves
integral parts. Economic activities based on reciprocal
help between categories of kin provided security in times
of disaster but did not make for individual ambition to
change conditions of life.[24] The new governments, especially that of Tanzania, wanted new economic attitudes
and philosophies, not the preservation of the past. Their
main difficulty is the cost of alternatives to the use of
traditional leaders. What is the economic outlay required for new settlement schemes in terms of skilled
supervisors, often expatriate managers at the present
time? What is the cost of a series of African technical
assistants in lieu of the old multipurpose leaders? What
would be the effect of armies of village activators and
peasant leaders with three weeks' training, as recommended by Dumont?[25] Can local branches of national
political parties, such as TANU, undertake economic
instruction and the inculcation of political ideas? These
are some of the problems which confront leaders of
multicultural states which I will discuss very briefly.

AGRICULTURAL POLICIES IN INDEPENDENT EAST AFRICA

Independence for the three East African states, in the
1960s, still left many of the problems of the rural economy unchanged. The road and rail system was still
inadequate, especially in Tanzania. There was the same

[24] See Jon Morris' statement that "The overall pattern was predicated
upon surviving the worst years and not upon maximising one's output
in the best." Rural Development Seminar at Dar-es-Salaam, April, 1966,
"The Educational Requirements of a Transformational Approach to
Agricultural Development" (Mimeographed by Tanzania Ministry of
Information and Tourism, Dar-es-Salaam).

[25] Dumont, *False Start*, pp. 204-6.

dispersal of the rural population, the problem of shifting cultivation, and the same small village settlements which made agricultural instruction and propaganda difficult to organize without a large rural staff. One has in fact to look at the date to be sure whether a document on rural development was written in 1945 or 1965. There was the same shortage of agricultural technicians, and in fact, the scarcity of trained manpower was even greater than before. Expatriate staff left; African senior civil servants of the middle range were quickly appointed in their place and there were serious gaps below. East Africa was probably shorter of specialist agricultural and engineering staff than West Africa. Its literacy rate was lower and the proportion of university-trained men and women to the rest of the population was not as high. Wealthy West Africans from the coastal areas had been sending their sons overseas for education long before the days of scholarships and bursaries which followed World War II. In East Africa, private fortunes of this kind were rare at the beginning of the century.

Against these disadvantages must be set the tremendous enthusiasm of the new rulers, their determination to modernize Africa at high speed, and the faith which has been able to move at least some of the mountains in the way of advance. Again, organizations able to tackle rural problems existed, at any rate in Tanzania. This country, unlike Kenya or Uganda, was able to build up a national political party, TANU. TANU had been in existence since 1948 and became a great political force in the elections of 1956. Unlike many modern African parties, TANU had made an early bid for local support. According to Friedland, "By 1959, a network of village organisations had been created which encompassed the entire country."[26] The village branchlets were used for economic as well as political purposes when the independence of Tanzania was declared.

The new East African states also had the advantage of being able to draw on wider financial resources than before. Though most of their outside funds still come from the United Kingdom, international agencies as well as other powers such as the United States, Germany, and China now contribute sizeable loans or grants. Thus, in 1964, the estimated total of grants and loans to Kenya from the United Kingdom reached £10.44 million and from other sources, £2.7 million. In the same year British grants and loans made to Uganda were £10.86 million and those from other sources came to £7.47 million.[27] The contribution of the great American foundations, especially to projects of African education and research, is very well known.

Perhaps more important in the long run was the fact that East African governments drew on many more different social philosophies and institutional patterns than the old colonial administrations had ever done. Ideas and even personnel for welfare schemes came from America, but also from Scandinavia, West and East Germany, China, and Israel.[28] A Tanzanian minister speaking at a seminar on rural development in Dar-es-Salaam in 1966 referred to the experience of collective

[26] W. H. Friedland, "Tanganyika's Political System" in *The Transformation of East Africa*, ed. Diamond and Burke, p. 296. The history of TANU is well described in this essay and works by M. Bates, "Tanganyika" in *African One-Party States*, ed. Gwen Carter (Ithaca: Cornell University Press, 1962) and by James Clagett Taylor, *The Political Development of Tanganyika* (Stanford: Stanford University Press, 1963).

[27] Krishna, pp. 272-73.

[28] Tanzania appointed an experienced Israeli, B. Yalan, to draw up its settlement policy in the first instance.

farms in Russia, of the kibbutzim in Israel, and of Japanese methods of increasing agricultural production. It would have been unusual for a British minister speaking to an agricultural audience in England to draw his examples from so wide a field. Young Africans still go to the United Kingdom for training, but also to America, China, Russia, Israel, Denmark, Germany, and Switzerland. There is a lively sense of experiment, especially perhaps in Tanzania.

The new governments' interest in the methods of rural development described—that is, forced cultivation, development schemes for special areas, model villages, plans for helping individual farmers—was first and foremost in *transformation* rather than *improvement*. They were in favour of building up new communities rather than ameliorating conditions in the old. Most Africans were deeply and irreversibly opposed to the retention of tribal divisions and the use of tribal authorities in their administrative programmes. They also were anxious to use the new settlements to teach or to express new ideas, and particularly to build up loyalties to the new central government in place of allegiance to tribal authorities. For both these reasons, they aimed at a central control greater than that exercised by the previous colonial governments, especially control over local appointments and the grants for local projects. The devolution of administrative powers to local authorities which had been a feature of British colonial policy after World War II was reversed, and the budgetary control they had been given as a means of "training Africans in local government" was rescinded. As in other parts of Africa, new administrative regions and districts were created, sometimes expressly in order to avoid the former coincidence between a cultural (tribal) region and a unit of local government. Provincial and district commissioners tended to be chosen from political party officials; they were considered responsible for ensuring loyalty to the central government, rather than officers engaged in the direct administration of welfare measures. In all these respects, the East African states differed little in practice from Ghana and other West African countries.

The experts from Europe and America invited to Africa to advise on social policy were also opposed to the retention of old cultural divisions as units of administration. Few of them had previous experience of African societies and the anthropological studies then available were not suitable for their purposes. Most of these advisers were economists who were consulted directly on the best means of increasing revenue, and not on the formation of healthy communities with the necessary indigenous leadership. In the first instance, the new advisers, whether economists, political scientists, or sociologists, naturally tended to recommend the institutions and practices familiar in their own countries, since these were the processes in which they were expert. They were highly specialized, whether in land registration, cooperative societies, rural industries, or marketing, and they naturally were interested in problems rather than people. The conflict of ideas between the traditional leaders, the idealistic central politicians, and the expatriate specialists has produced much agonizing reappraisal and an apparent volte-face in Tanzania recently.

Uganda has stuck mainly to improvement policies, apart from some small settlement schemes such as some tea cultivation farms in Ankole. Kenya had already embarked on large settlements of the Swynnerton type before the declaration of independence and the opening of the scheduled areas in the former white highlands made new land available for peasant settlement or large-scale farming by wealthy Africans. The increase in production has been remarkable in some areas,[29] but it is difficult to know how far the new settlements still depend on expatriate management and how far a genuinely indigenous leadership and sense of community has developed to take its place. The cost of the schemes in terms of initial capital and expert staff has been large, over £11 million in the case of the initial Swynnerton scheme.

Tanzania is the state which has made the most experiments and where the basic issues are most clearly revealed. The government's big settlement programme was announced by the President in 1962. It was certainly intended as part of an economic policy. It was hoped, for instance, that settlement in river basins would relieve overcrowding and that encouragement of new village communities would put an end to shifting cultivation. But the political philosophy behind the economic plan was evident from the start. Tanzania wanted transformation methods rather than improvements. In Tanzania's first five-year plan, one of the stated aims was "to short-cut the slow pace of traditional extension efforts"[30] and to move ahead more quickly. Community effort was in line with Julius Nyerere's form of socialism. It was also viewed as part of a "distinctively African past" which was and is "intrinsically 'good' and can be isolated, updated,

[29] The median income of peasants settled at Mweiga was three times that expected, as shown by Wilson Nguyo, quoted in Jon Morris, p. 11.

[30] The United Republic of Tanganyika and Zanzibar, *Five-Year Plan for Economic and Social Development, July 1964—June 1969*, Vol. I, pp. 21-23, Vol. II, p. 27.

and utilised to contribute towards a productive, dignified, and modern way of life"[31]—a policy strongly reminiscent of the British missionaries' desire "to preserve the best in African life" and based perhaps on the same nostalgia. Settlements were also founded with political objectives in mind—to secure "political penetration" and to "bring people into the authoritative communication network of the political system through the local T.A.N.U."[32] authorities—that is, to strengthen the ties of the peasant with the central rather than the local traditional government. The settlements were to have an expert manager and a staff, all appointed by the central, not the local government. In fact, many Tanzanian politicians "tend to believe that parochial and traditional interests are *ipso facto* illegitimate."[33] There was to be a cooperative society in each community. Peasant farmers were to receive thirty shillings a month subsistence and full food during the first year and were to repay the loans on the scheme over twenty-five years. It was hoped they would make £150 a year, a 50 per cent increase on the national average.

The settlement scheme was ambitious. It was hoped to found seventy-four pilot schemes by 1969 and to have settled half a million people by 1980, a quarter million in the Wami river area and another quarter million in village settlements at Urambo, Rachengat, Kongwa, and

[31] One of the six guidelines for rural development announced by the Tanzanian authorities, quoted by John Nelles in a paper entitled "Planning for Public Support," read to the 1966 Rural Development Seminar; see n. 26.

[32] Garry Thomas, "Effects of New Communities in Rural Areas—The Upper Kitete Example," read to the 1966 Rural Development Seminar; see n. 24.

[33] E. S. Brack Brown, "Development Administration and Implementation," paper read to the Rural Development Seminar; see n. 24.

78

Matongoro. The schemes were planned to absorb 13.5 per cent of the whole development budget.[34]

Actually the total number of settlements was far in excess of those planned. Four major pilot schemes came into existence quickly, those at Mtale, Rwankoma, Upper Kitete, Kingorungundwa; seven settlements were taken over from the former Tanganyika Agricultural Corporation; and three were former Agricultural Development schemes. There were also six Israeli management schemes, apparently of the kibbutz type, receiving some financial help, and a great variety and number of small group farms awarded help from regional funds.[35]

The year 1965 was one of anxious appraisal and a final retreat from this ambitious policy. The story is a familiar one under African conditions. Here, as elsewhere, the capital costs of settlement had proved too high. Estimates were in the range of £150,000 per 250 families. A number of the projects were under expensive, expatriate management with supervision by expert African technicians. The indebtedness of the farmers was proving too great a burden and, as the President pointed out, trained agricultural personnel, so pitifully short in Tanzania, was being tied up in work for privileged communities. The schemes in fact were disappointing in terms of socialist philosophy as well as economics. The privileged communities proved to be less enthusiastic than volunteers because they had come to expect more from the government,[36] and it was feared that the farmers

[34] See Carol Fisher, "Tanzania Settlement," *Venture* 19, no. 6 (1967) (London: Fabian Colonial Bureau, 1967).

[35] Tanzania, Commission on Agricultural Development, *Report* (Dar-es-Salaam: Government Printer, 1965) mentions four to five hundred of these.

[36] See Fisher and also Robert Chambers, *New Society*, October 13, 1966.

were, or were becoming, a specially favoured class. Nyerere had in fact come up against another, almost universal problem in Africa, or in any region which wants to develop fast: the problem of how to encourage advance where advance is possible, without creating a privileged class.

The retreat from the settlement policy was almost complete. By an announcement made in April 1966, the government ended grants for new schemes, announced the closure of those that were not viable, and described its new policy as "piece-meal modernisation of existing traditional villages" by such steps as reorganizing land-holdings and layout, planning better water supplies and farming improvements. Significantly, too, the new policy was "to sponsor the creation of an active organisation by the people under their own leaders, for carrying out the work." It is not clear whether the phrase "the people under their own leaders" is intended to describe traditional leaders or local TANU officials. Perhaps both are intended, since there is probably considerable overlap between the two nowadays.[37]

It might appear that Tanzania is back to something like the old colonial policy of slow improvement of peasant agriculture through local leaders, who are part of and animated by the same values as the community, using familiar sanctions and decision-making processes. But has the Tanzanian government been forced by its poverty, its want of technical staff, and its scattered population to use the traditional authorities it wanted to by-pass? The situation has, I think, changed more radically

---

[37] Garry Thomas reports that the leader of some of the activities in the pilot scheme village of Upper Kitete performed some of the socializing, adjudicative, and ceremonial functions of the traditional Iraqw elders. See n. 32.

than this. The government has destroyed the bigger tribal administrative divisions, such as the chiefdom and the sub-chiefdom, which are out of line with its nation-building policy, but it will have to use the local village authorities and to concentrate on training and advising these, perhaps turning them into village activators in Dumont's sense. This may be slow, but changes so accomplished will have a chance of becoming permanent and will not be dependent on outside managerial staff, expatriate or African. They will not necessarily be limited to privileged pilot villages. Tanzania's experiment has also concentrated thought and research on the lower levels of administration, the micro-politics level, so far avoided by most political scientists in Africa. In this, the government's officials seem to have been aided and stimulated by the imaginative research of the East African Studies Program of Syracuse University, which sent to Tanzania a mixed team of political scientists, sociologists, anthropologists, economists, and others. They engaged in field research in sample communities and in joint policy discussions with the government, and with the University at Dar-es-Salaam organized the Rural Development Seminar in 1966.

Anthropologists have an important part to play at this micro-political level, though British fieldworkers at any rate have not been interested in such problems of recent years. They could provide more quickly than any other social scientist what Margaret Read called so long ago a "sociological map" of an area in which change is intended.[38] But they could also contribute to the science of development administration by small-scale studies of village leadership, formal and informal; types of kinship

[38] Great Britain, Colonial Office, *Memorandum on Mass Education in Africa,* Col. No. 186 (London: HMSO, 1943).

as a basis for corporate action; processes of decision-making in relation to new practices; the relation between education and incentives in economic life; and social mobility and capital formation. The East African states include many tribes, some of them very small, but they do fall into something like the types described in Chapter I. These have tended to react very differently to new economic changes, and insufficient comparative work has been done on this subject at the village level.[39] Such work might provide many stimulating ideas for the development experts. It would also show the vitality of many cultures at the lower village and district level, a fact for which modern African policy makers may well come to be grateful at this stage of their history.

[39] See Richards, *East African Chiefs*, chap. 15, and Fred G. Burke, *Local Government and Politics in Uganda* (Syracuse: Syracuse University Press, 1964).

CHAPTER IV:
INTEGRATING FORCES

THE diversity of the many small societies of East Africa has been the subject of the first part of this book. In contrast, our final chapter attempts to list the integrating forces now at work in this region. Integration here includes the administrative machinery for joint action between members of different cultures and different states, and the habits of cooperation based on such machinery. The different measures taken to promote common ideas and political ambitions in the new states and the sense of identity their citizens have developed will also be discussed.

These are difficult issues to describe briefly. The ambitions of African politicians are large. They continually amaze the inhabitants of the Old World. Most of them are struggling to achieve integration at three levels simultaneously, that is, within their own territories, within large regions such as West or East Africa, and even in the continent of Africa as a whole. Alfred the Great and his successors who tried to unite an England composed of many small polities were not attempting at the same time to produce an integrated Europe; yet African leaders in their own continent are attempting a task of just this magnitude. Some of the forces making for unity at these three levels of integration can be described, but obviously only in a very superficial way.

One difficulty is the lack of up-to-date information.

African visions of united territories and a united continent have been described and discussed for over a century. They originated mainly in West Africa, where the contact with European colonial powers has been so much longer than in the East and where the influence of men of African descent from America and the West Indies has been so strong. Letters, diaries, and newspaper articles on African political aspirations date from the founding of the two colonies of repatriated slaves— Sierra Leone (1787) and Liberia (1822). This literature is in fact very copious. But the implementation of these ideas had to wait for the coming of independence and is therefore very recent; nine years in the case of Ghana and three in that of Kenya. Newspapers certainly give fuller coverage of African affairs now than in the colonial period, in spite of press censorship in some states. Conferences are frequent and provide reports; politicians' speeches are published as well as their biographies, autobiographies, and philosophical statements. But it is still too soon to gauge the extent to which the new ideas are accepted at the district and village level, or the type of balance which has been reached between the newer forces of unity and the tribal rivalries described earlier.

The history of the spread to East Africa of the Pan-Africanism of West African politicians has not been fully documented yet, but special characteristics of the political philosophy of this region begin to emerge.

TERRITORIAL INTEGRATION

In the years preceding independence, the sense of common identity in East Africa depended on four different factors: the unifying force of anticolonial, anti-British feeling among the élite; the habits of cooperation developed through membership in the various national legislatures set up by the British in anticipation of independence; the territorial viewpoint fostered in African members of the central civil service; and, in the case of Tanzania, a single national party.

Anticolonial feeling was a force for unity in every part of Africa which had been under colonial rule.

National legislatures and national assemblies could not be called truly African until the coming of independence. There were special difficulties over introducing universal suffrage in East Africa because of the presence of very substantial and powerful European and Asian minorities, especially in Kenya and Tanzania (see Chapter I). Though the British authorities assumed that their ex-colonies would have governments of an entirely British type—that is to say, parliamentary government based on universal suffrage, with ministers drawn from the political party which had gained the majority at an election—this was difficult to achieve in East Africa since they insisted on reserved seats for the European and Asian minorities.[1] Yet once there was a sizeable body of Africans elected from separate constituencies, a group of national politicians came into being. Leaders from backward districts probably participated in central politics for the first time. In Uganda those from the advanced districts frankly said, after the opening of the National Assembly, that this was the first time they had met representatives from the north or northwest of their own country. Many of them had visited Europe and America several times but they had not travelled within their own territory. Learning the parliamentary procedure

[1] Tanzania's Legislative Council of 1960 was composed of 52 Africans, 13 Asians, 16 Europeans, and 10 nominated members. In Kenya, the Legislative Council of 1961 contained 53 common roll seats of which 20 were reserved for minorities—10 Europeans, 8 Asians, and 2 Arabs—and 12 national seats.

and the rules for debate and question-time, as well as the continuity of association achieved by periodic meetings, seemed to produce a sense of expertise and a tradition which was especially valued, according to my personal observations, by members from remote districts. Though the new constitutions of these countries were quickly changed after independence—within a year in Kenya, and four years in Uganda—the importance of these new habits of cooperation should not be underestimated.

In the central civil service, Africans who took over senior posts from Europeans seem to have retained the territorial as distinct from the local outlook. To my knowledge, an analysis of the ethnic affiliations of the men in these posts has not been made recently. The greatly increased control of the local by the central governments in all the three territories has already been described (see Chapter III).

All three territories, with Zanzibar now united to Tanzania, have become one-party states and this of course can make for a sense of unity. In Tanzania, TANU has been in power since the elections of 1958; Kenya was declared a one-party state in August 1964, after achieving independence the previous December. Uganda is controlled by the UPC but it is not clear that a formal pronouncement of a one-party constitution has been made. We are probably too close to the recent changes in East Africa to be able to know whether a sense of national unity now exists in the minds of the ordinary man and woman in these territories, the man in the banana gardens and on the cattle-covered hillside. When the singing, the dancing, and the fireworks of the *Uhuru* celebrations were over, what feeling of identification with the new state remained?

Kenyatta and Nyerere have both become national symbols; Obote, in his more difficult situation, has not. Kenyatta has been transformed from an anticolonial hero to a father-figure in Kenya. Nyerere's strong character and cult of simplicity and equality has given him a unique place in the history of Tanzania and indeed of Africa as a whole. Obote has had to face rival political symbols in the form of four traditional kings.

Slogans such as *uhuru* (freedom) and *umoja* (unity) have been used widely in speeches and in party literature in both Kenya and Tanzania. Later the emphasis was rather on hard work for the country. Nyerere, for instance, talks of *uhuru na kazi* (freedom and work); and Kenya makes great use of the cry *harambee* (pull together). Statements of their particular brand of African socialism have been slower to appear, though Nyerere has had a constant political philosophy and has made important speeches on the subject, usually at annual TANU meetings.[2] Kenyatta's statement on "African Socialism and its Application to Planning in Kenya" was widely distributed in leaflet form.[3] The teaching of both these leaders is much less explicit than that used by Mao Tse-tung in indoctrinating Chinese peasants, though the utterances of Nyerere seem to have turned from party statements to the announcement of a definite philosophy. It would be interesting to know what form of

[2] Julius Nyerere, *Ujamaa, the Basis of African Socialism* (TANU publication, 1962); *Democracy and the Party System* (Dar-es-Salaam: Tanganyika Standard Limited, n.d.). *The Arusha Declaration* (Dar-es-Salaam, Government Printer, 1967), made at the National Executive Committee of TANU at the Community Centre, Arusha, 1967, is the most explicit of all.

[3] Jomo Kenyatta, *African Socialism and its Application to Planning in Kenya* (Nairobi: Government Printer, 1965). (Reprinted by the African Centre Ltd., London.)

political teaching goes on in the schools of Kenya and Tanzania and at their village party meetings, but this would require special research.

All African politicians have the difficult task of building up a sense of common tradition in territories in which the population is heterogeneous. Which culture are they to select as the basis of a unitary set of values and a common history? McKim Marriott makes a fascinating comparison between the positions of India, Pakistan, Ceylon, Burma, and Africa in this respect, describing them all as countries faced with "the choice of suitable pasts."[4] Ghana under Nkrumah tried to create "a unitary supertribal myth" mainly by adopting symbols and ritual from the dominant kingdom of Ashanti.[5] "Links to illustrious if obscure empires of history" are stressed as part of the common tradition in both Ghana and Mali.[6]

In East Africa, the position is more difficult still. A common tradition of the struggle against colonialism is a unifying factor in all parts of Africa which have been under foreign rule, but school textbooks have not yet been rewritten from this point of view. The literate tradition associated in West Africa with early Moslem penetration was not an important factor in the Eastern territories. Nor could it give the same depth of history as Ghana and Mali, for instance, have achieved through the use of Moslem records. Tanzania has no dominant culture like that of the Ashanti kingdom in Ghana. Kenya has a number of age-set societies which have a

4 McKim Marriott, "Cultural Policy in the New States," in *Old Societies and New States,* ed. Clifford Geertz (New York: Free Press of Glencoe, 1963), p. 51.

5 *Ibid.,* p. 28.

6 *Ibid.,* p. 51.

good deal in common but this traditional structure has not been cited. The traditions and symbols of the ancient kingdoms of Uganda are not likely to be adopted as a basis for a unitary tradition of Uganda by a government which has just destroyed these kingdoms. The whole question of historical traditions for East Africa will be referred to again under the contribution of East African universities.

REGIONAL COOPERATION

Regional integration has been more successful in East Africa than in West. In fact, at one time it looked as though a genuine federation of the three great territories and Zanzibar would be achieved. West Africa is of course split into English- and French-speaking territories which have had administrations of a British or French type, and this has made cooperation much more difficult than in the East.[7] Again, Nkrumah, the dominant figure in West African politics at one time, opposed regional associations strongly because he thought they would stand in the way of his dream of a united Africa. Senghor took the same attitude. The East African territories are poorer and therefore the economic advantages of integration have perhaps struck them more forcibly. They have been under European rule or influence for a shorter time and are perhaps more open to suggestions for new types of administration, and have fewer vested interests in different political and economic enterprises.

[7] The union of Guinea and Ghana was achieved in 1958 but its success seems to have been transitory. An *entente* between four French territories—Upper Volta, Dahomey, Niger, and the Ivory Coast—was attempted in the same year. A Brazzaville group of twelve French territories set up headquarters in Brazzaville in 1960, but the union lapsed during the Congo wars.

89

The history of regional planning in East Africa is a long one. Sir Harry Johnston recommended the amalgamation of Kenya and Uganda as long ago as 1899.[8] The attempts to reach closer union between the territories took two forms in the preindependence period. The first can be described as a continuous attempt on the part of the colonial governments to get closer cooperation in technical fields so as to pool the resources of these rather poor territories and thus to effect financial savings. These efforts were first opposed by African politicians, and specially those from Buganda, for political reasons. They were afraid that any form of East African federation would be dominated by Kenya with its powerful white settler minority. The second campaign for closer union was that organized by African politicians themselves, again mainly with political motives. They wanted to build up a great federation of East African states which would be powerful enough to resist the dangers of "re-colonisation" and to ensure itself a place on world councils. This movement of African leaders was not confined to British territories but included Ethiopia, Somalia, and other states.

Many of the colonial governments' plans for technical cooperation have been implemented. A number of commissions have considered the problems involved. An East African Commission under Ormsby-Gore, in 1925,[9] recommended periodic conferences of the governors of the three territories, and the first of these was held in 1926. Some cooperation over trade, customs, and postal services followed. In 1929, the Hilton-Young Commission on Closer Union also reported on the need for more

8 Kenneth Ingham, *A History of East Africa* (London: Longmans, Green, 1962), p. 207.

9 Great Britain, Colonial Office, *Report of the East Africa Commission 1925*, Cmd. 2387 (London: HMSO, 1925).

regional cooperation, and this was followed by a Joint Select Committee in 1931.[10] All three Commissions considered a federation of the three East African territories and Zanzibar to be impossible at the time. Then, as now, economic cooperation was seen to be desirable, but individual governments did not want to give up their existing plans for development.

However, in 1948 an East African High Commission was finally set up in Nairobi and was given responsibility for a number of interterritorial services such as railways, customs, post and telegraph, income tax, research, and statistics. It remained in operation until 1961, the year that the Raisman Economic and Fiscal Commission reported on the possibilities of an East African Currency Board and an East African Common Market.[11] The High Commission was transformed that year into an East African Common Services organization, the title being considered more consonant with the sovereignty of Tanzania, which had become independent in 1961.[12]

Interterritorial cooperation in the technical field, therefore, was well advanced, and federation was in sight. In fact, a meeting of the East African Conference, a body which met periodically and was composed of the governors of the three territories and the Resident of Zanzibar with thirteen territorial representatives, held a meeting in Nairobi in January 1961, and this conference actually

10 Great Britain, Colonial Office, *Report of the Commission on Closer Union of the Dependencies in Eastern and Central Africa* (Hilton-Young Commission), Cmd. 3234 (London: HMSO, 1929). *Joint Select Committee on East Africa, Minutes of Evidence* (London: HMSO, 1931).

11 Great Britain, Colonial Office, *East Africa: Report of the Economic and Fiscal Commission* (Raisman Report), Cmnd. 1279 (London: HMSO, 1961).

12 A. Rweyemamu and Brack Brown, "Federation: An Unfinished Portrait," in *The Transformation of East Africa*, ed. Stanley Diamond and Fred G. Burke (New York: Basic Books, 1966), p. 585.

envisaged a federation of the East African territories by 1964.

Nyerere, however, was deeply conscious of the suspicions of African politicians regarding any form of federation planned by colonial authorities and possibly dominated by Europeans. He urged that independence should be granted to the three territories simultaneously so that the new governments could start their existence within a federation before they had developed their own policies and programmes.[13] Intertribal tensions and conflict made this impossible in the case of Kenya and Uganda, and four independent governments were set up one after the other: Tanzania in 1961, Uganda in 1962, Kenya and Zanzibar in 1963.

The African politicians' own organization for regional cooperation dated from 1958, when PAFMECA, the Pan-African Freedom Movement of East and Central Africa, held its first meeting in September at Addis Ababa and subsequently proceeded with great energy and drive to hold a series of meetings: in Zanzibar (April 1959), in Moshi (December 1959), at Nairobi and at Mbale in 1960, and at Addis Ababa again in 1962. These were not meetings for the discussion of government machinery but for the association of East and also Central African leaders with common political aims. Ghana had attained independence in 1957 and the PAFMECA leaders were determined to fight for the liberation of other African territories, not only the British colonies and Trust territory, but also the Portuguese territories and the whole of South Africa. PAFMECA was remarkable for its wide membership. It included the three East African territories as well as Zanzibar, Zambia, Malawi, and Ethiopia. Later, it was joined by Somalia. In 1962, it changed its

[13] *Ibid.*

name from PAFMECA to PAFMECSA to include South African delegates. It was remarkable also for the variety of different polities represented; the delegates included the emperor of an ancient Christian kingdom, a Moslem sultan of Zanzibar, and the head of a Bantu kingdom in Uganda, together with the leader of the national populist party of Tanzania, and a politician–trade-unionist from Kenya.

The high ambitions of the delegates were impressive. Mboya, flying to Addis Ababa from a Kenya rent by tribal party divisions, still seemed able to visualize a regional union of these very diverse states. Politicians in Uganda who were unable to reach a compromise between militant Buganda and the rest of the country still apparently thought it possible to achieve an East African federation. States without armies discussed the overthrow of the South African government. The whole series of PAFMECSA conferences reflected the longing of African politicians to build up large and powerful states. PAFMECSA faded away in May 1963, when the new Organization of African Unity (OAU) was set up in its final form and took over the campaign for the liberation of the parts of Africa which were still under foreign rule, and when the governments of the three East African territories set up working parties to make their own detailed plans for federation. It was certainly a most enterprising venture while it lasted, and it paved the way for much future cooperation.

After the summit conference was over, the delegates from the three East African territories held a further meeting in March, and on 5 June passed a Declaration of Federation which was to come into effect by the end of 1963. The news was hailed with enthusiasm inside Africa and without. Working parties on a possible federal constitution followed with the utmost rapidity: on 9 June at Dar-es-Salaam, on 29 June at Kampala, and on 10 August at Dar-es-Salaam again.[14] But difficulties were already apparent. The site of the new capital, the nature of the new central legislature, and the division of functions between the federal and the territorial authority were all subjects of controversy, as they have been in the case of other federations. Uganda had become hostile and by the last meeting (20 September 1963) it was clear that federation was not an immediate possibility. The governments of Tanzania and Zanzibar amalgamated on their own in April 1964. Cooperation on the economic issues between all four territories and the East African Common Service Union remains.

AFRICA AS A UNIT

Pan-African movements of the late nineteenth and early twentieth century were of American and West African origin rather than East African. They were organized mainly by men who had been neither born nor educated in the continent for which they dreamed and planned, and they were often ignorant of its practical problems. W. E. B. DuBois, who organized the first Pan-African Conference at Philadelphia in 1900, was an American citizen; H. Sylvester, who helped him, was a West Indian. Marcus Garvey, the famous Pan-Africanist who at one time proclaimed himself provisional president of a "Racial Empire" in Africa, also came from the West Indies. George Padmore, a tireless worker for African unity, was another West Indian. Aimé Césaire, the French poet who figured prominently in the *Présence Africaine* movement of later years, was born in Martinique.

14 *Ibid.;* for a detailed account of these working parties, pp. 587, 592.

The first Pan-African conferences were held in America (1920, 1927) or Europe (1919, 1922, 1923, and 1949) and not in Africa.[15] In fact, the first meeting of this sort to be held on African soil was the Conference of Independent African States in Cairo (April 1958) followed by the All-African Peoples Conference at Accra in December 1958, the year after Ghana had become independent. These conferences were attended by delegates not only from Africa, but also from many other countries such as America, the West Indies, India, China, and other parts of Asia. In fact, there were representatives from groups all over the world who were, or had been, under white domination or who came from underprivileged minorities living in white societies. In the first instance, the delegates voiced passionate protests against the treatment of coloured men all over the world and tried to band themselves together to assert their dignity and to proclaim their common race. They apparently did not discuss machinery for the constitution of a United States of Africa; nor were they much concerned with fighting for the independence of colonial territories in Africa, a possibility which must have seemed very far off in the first quarter of this century. Little time seems to have been given to the internal political and social problems of these territories. For instance, Indians were present at the conferences, and though there are large minorities of Asians in East Africa, as we have seen, there is no record of Indians and Africans combining in political action against their European rulers under the influence of the Pan-African movement. These early meetings protested and organized support, but they did

15 Rayford W. Logan, "The Historical Aspects of Pan-Africanism 1900-45," in *Pan-Africanism Reconsidered*, ed. American Society of African Culture (Berkeley and Los Angeles: University of California Press, 1962), p. 8.

not engage in practical action. In fact, it sometimes seems as though Africa was a political concept to these first Pan-Africanists, rather than a political actuality—a vision of a continent free and united, with its divisions healed, its internal boundaries removed, its power recognized by the rest of the world, and above all the black man everywhere in control.

East African leaders of course were affected by the discussions of the Pan-African conferences and particularly by those of later years. But they entered the arena at a time when independence obviously was imminent in many parts of Africa and when urgent political problems presented themselves. The influence of Pan-Africanists from America and the West Indies, with their more distant and unrealistic visions, was never an important factor in East African politics. In 1958, when Nyerere and other East African delegates attended the Conference of Independent States in Cairo and the All-African Peoples Conference at Accra, active plans for the setting-up of political machinery were already under discussion. Events were moving rapidly. At the Lagos meeting (January 1962), a permanent secretariat was discussed; at a Tunis meeting (April 1962), a declaration of noninterference in the affairs of member states was adopted. At the third Summit Conference of Independent African States, held in Addis Ababa in 1963, thirteen leaders of African territories agreed on a Charter for the Organization of African Unity (OAU) already described. The trained diplomats of Europe would not, and probably could not, have moved so quickly!

With the fall of Nkrumah, the strongest supporter of the concept of a United States of Africa, active campaigning for the political unity of the continent seems to have lapsed though the cooperation over common issues has increased. Support for Africans under alien rule in South Africa, the Portuguese territories, and Rhodesia is one such issue, and one for which the East and Central African states have assumed special responsibility, perhaps because this effort is in direct line with the activities of PAFMECSA.[16]

The OAU now has its own secretariat. It has made important political declarations of intent. It has also made several attempts to settle interterritorial disputes. The Nigerian-Biafran war is the most important of these cases, and it is a measure of the undoubted authority of the OAU that it definitely has been asked by European powers such as Great Britain to intervene, to mediate, and to conduct peace talks. It is surely a considerable achievement to have reached such a standing since 1963.

But if Pan-Africanism proper has receded into the background at the moment, there is one aspect of the United Africa concept which affects all African states alike: that is the attempt by some of the leading politicians to prove that the inhabitants of the whole continent have a unique and common culture, an African personality, an African philosophy and art, or a *présence Africaine*. It is easy to understand the need for such a belief. The dilemma of the African élite in every state is quite plain. Until recently, all its leaders had been educated in British, French, and Portuguese-type schools and often in European and American universities. They have naturally adopted western values and standards of living. For a hundred years and more, these standards have been the measure of their achievement, their "civilization,"

16 The nine-member African Liberation Committee responsible for trying to free countries still ruled by Europeans has its headquarters at Dar-es-Salaam.

and their equality with the rest of the world. Their acceptance has been in fact the common bond uniting the élite.

Yet with nationalist feeling running as high as it does, dependence on the West is the last thing African leaders want to assert. Hence the two mutually exclusive views in so many of their speeches and policy statements. On the one hand, African states are to be modernized as quickly as possible. Tribal divisions and tribal administrations are to be swept away and with them the heavy obligations of traditional kinship, felt to be crippling to individual enterprise. Industry of the most modern and sophisticated type is to be introduced as rapidly as possible. Nkrumah, for instance, used to demand "jet-age development," not merely quick development. But on the other hand, these very leaders feel a deep emotional need to reject things European and hence to glorify their own cultures and to prove that these are as admirable as the civilizations of Europe, or superior to them.[17] The difficulties of selecting a single cultural background for each new state have been described. To find common features in the many civilizations of Africa, from the Kalahari bushmen to the kingdoms of Dahomey, Benin, and Buganda, is a harder task still. Some of the leaders of the *Présence Africaine* movement go further still and associate a spiritual unity among all men and women with a black skin, wherever they may be found in the world.

There have been three major arguments used in the attempt to bridge the gap between European or American cultures adopted by the élite and the African cultures in which they live or came to live. The first is the

---

[17] Comparisons with Asian civilizations do not seem to have been made though these would have been instructive and stimulating.

position taken by the eminent West African leaders of
the mid-nineteenth century, many of them expatriates
from America or the West Indies as we have seen, and
in some cases returning to the country of their birth after
battling in West Africa for many years. The contrast
between the culture they had left and the country to
which they had come looking for freedom and oppor-
tunity must have been striking and often distressing.
Many of these Negro leaders were Christian ministers,
since this was one of the few professions in which a black
man could rise to some semblance of social status in the
America of the time. It is not surprising that they found
"African customs" alien and disreputable and felt it
their business to change them as quickly as possible. By
the Liberian Constitution of 1847, citizenship was to be
granted only to those who had "abandoned all the forms,
customs, and superstitions of heathenism and . . . con-
formed to the forms, customs, and habits of civilised
life."[18] Negro intellectuals from French-speaking areas
were even more emphatic. Boileau, a French priest
trained in France who founded a secondary school in
St. Louis (1843), spoke of those "gross, if not dishonour-
able ways known as the *custom of the country*,"[19] and
Holle, the Creole explorer and soldier from Senegal, a
great opponent of the Moslem faith, exclaimed, "Let us
have no more talk of toleration and religious freedom!"[20] This is a far cry from the glorification of things
African to be found in the current movement of the
Présence Africaine.

Indeed, the attitude of the first African leaders was
definitely missionary. They accepted as fact that the

[18] R. W. July, *The Origins of Modern African Thought* (London:
Faber & Faber, 1967), p. 100.
[19] *Ibid.*, p. 160.
[20] *Ibid.*, p. 172.

traditional cultures of their beloved continent were at the moment inferior to those of the West, but claimed that they could be raised to the accepted level with outside help. Africans could then be integrated into the civilized world and belong to it. In particular, they would become part of Christendom. East African leaders were not of New World origin, but they were mainly Christians and they expressed similar points of view. In Buganda, Apolo Kagwa and his fellow chiefs, who had all become Christians, were particularly severe on any signs of survival of pagan belief.

Later in the century, West African leaders began to assert the equality of African peoples in every sphere of European achievement. This was done by citing cases of individual African successes in every part of the continent. But white men still remained the reference group: it was their achievements which remained the touchstone of success throughout. W. E. Abraham, an African nationalist from Ghana and a great admirer of Nkrumah, writing in 1961 and describing the advanced nature of the culture of the Akan people, says that "they threw their cloths over one shoulder in the manner of the ancient Greeks."[21] He does not say that the ancient Greeks were civilized because they dressed like the Akan!

The desire of the African élite to compete in the European stakes has lasted nearly a century. It accounts for their determination to prove themselves by taking overseas examinations in the years before independence, and their bitter resentment at any attempt to alter school or university curricula to meet their local needs, for example by omitting Latin and Greek from the courses offered. Nkrumah and other African politicians, after taking power, began to accuse the colonial governments

21 W. E. Abraham, *The Mind of the African* (London: Weidenfeld and Nicolson, 1961), p. 87.

of preventing Africans from studying their indigenous history, languages, and cultures. In fact, however, it was the expert committees of the Colonial Office and the expatriate staff of African institutions of higher learning who urged the adaptation of curricula to local needs and sought to further African studies there. Overseas anthropologists of the thirties and later certainly ploughed a very lone furrow when they pressed for further studies of African societies in those countries.

In the mid-nineteenth century, the effort to prove that Africans as individuals could equal the achievements of the West went a step further. Both Edward Blyden and Africanus Horton claimed that many African societies had had a civilization similar to those of Europe even though they had lost it. They had introduced many of the arts into the more backward areas to the north of them. The black scholars of West Africa in the nineteenth century were of course trained like their European and African counterparts in the classical tradition. Events in the history of Athens, Rome, and Carthage were more familiar to them than those of the African past. Africanus Horton (1866) claimed that Africa was once so civilized that it attracted Greeks to its centres of learning. It preserved the civilization of Rome when its capital city fell. It provided many early Christian fathers of the Church.[22] Blyden, first professor of Latin and Greek in Liberia College (Monrovia) pointed out that the African continent had cradled two civilizations, Christianity and Islam; and that it had produced the marvel of the pyramids and other wonders.[23]

Nkrumah adopted this point of view nearly a century later. The famous frescoes which he had painted on the walls of the great hall of the Convention People's Party

[22] July, p. 116.
[23] *Ibid.*, p. 218.

CARL A. R̶ ̶ ̶L̶ ̶ ̶ LIBRARY
LENOIR RHYNE COLLEGE

(CPP) headquarters at Accra show "Africans" (Egyptians) inventing chemistry, medicine, architecture, mathematics, the making of paper, the alphabet, and shorthand, and teaching these arts to Europeans, mainly Greeks. As Nkrumah said, "All the glory of Egypt belongs to Africa and her people."[24] But the originators of the arts and the sciences in the CPP frescoes have the features of present-day West Africans and not of ancient Egyptians.

The third claim made by African politician-philosophers is perhaps the most interesting since it abandons the black-white competition and asserts boldly that Africans have a culture of their own, uniquely and entirely theirs—an African personality or a *présence Africaine.* To hold this view, it is of course necessary to look at the infinite diversity of African cultures with a telescope perpetually fixed to a blind eye. The diversity did not trouble the nineteenth-century politicians of Liberia and Sierra Leone, expatriate or indigenous, since they were generally unaware of the magnitude of the ethnic differences involved. Those were not the days when African Studies centres were scattered widely all over the world as they are now.

Blyden was most anxious to prove that Africans had a special contribution to make to the world and attempted to describe this contribution. He is said to have been the first writer to use the term "African personality." But the campus of Monrovia must have seemed worlds away from the "savage" interior of Liberia, and Blyden seems to have drawn as much from his knowledge of Greek and Roman society as from facts he knew or heard about African institutions. His aim was of course mainly

24 Nkrumah's opening address to the Congress of Africanists in Accra (1963), reprinted in *Présence Africaine,* 17, no. 45 (1963):15.

political. He lived in an era of nationalist philosophy. If there was no national concept in Africa, it was necessary to invent one. "No people," he writes, "can rise to an influential position among the nations without a distinct and efficient nationality. Cosmopolitanism has never affected anything."[25] He lists what he considers to be the national characteristics of Africans, such as the family basis of society, plural marriage, ownership of land, customs of mutual help, a natural inclination for religion, a power of sympathetic communion with the environment, and a pleasure in work evinced by the African habit of singing when at labour! Yet in spite of his insistence that Africans have a culture that is unique, and his view, then most unpopular, that they required a different type of education from that suited to Europeans, his proposed curriculum did not include any study of African history or cultures as such. His special African courses merely included the teaching of the ancient classics with the addition of Arabic and native languages, art, and music.[26]

The much more recent concept of the *présence Africaine*, almost entirely the creation of French-speaking Africans, first attracted publicity at a conference of black writers and artists at the Sorbonne in 1956, the *Congrès Internationale des Ecrivains et Artistes Noirs*. This movement has a permanent headquarters in Paris, organized by Alioune Diop, and publishes its own journal. Senghor, Césaire, and Sartre are among its eminent supporters. Here again, the emphasis is on the uniqueness of the African contribution to the world, but with a glorification of African culture not to be found among the nineteenth-century writers, a triumphant acceptance

[25] Quoted by July, p. 214.
[26] *Ibid.*, p. 227.

of blackness and of what Sartre calls "the black soul." Césaire's term is *négritude*. *Présence Africaine* gives the artist's picture of African thought and feeling as he sees them. It makes no reference, or very little reference, to the empirical studies of the history and institutions of the different ethnic groups in this enormous continent. The African, according to Senghor for instance, has a heightened sensibility, strong, uninhibited emotions, and an individualism which is outflowing, exuberant, and dionysiac.[27] These are artists' impressions of the culture and personality type familiar to social anthropologists, and particularly to those of the United States.

Concepts such as *négritude* do not seem to have appealed so strongly to the East African élite as they have done in West Africa. East African leaders seem much closer to the daily life of the common man and his institutions than do his counterparts in West Africa, and particularly to those of francophone Africa where the *évolués* had a different type of citizenship from the masses and a very different way of life, according to the French colonial policy. Also there is an exuberance of art forms, whether wood carving or textiles, to be found in the Negro cultures from West Africa and the Congo which has excited many European artists and has proved to the hilt the claim that Africans have made a special contribution to the world of art. A certain similarity of symbol and design has also supported the belief that these art forms are universal in the continent and that they constitute a proof that there is a black culture. But in East Africa wood carving has never been developed to this extent; nor has the weaving and dying of textiles. It is, therefore, easy to understand that a movement founded by artists reared in the tradition of West and

27 S. W. Allen, "Negritude: Agreement and Disagreement," in *Pan-Africanism Reconsidered*, p. 313.

Central African art should have less to say to the élite of
East Africa.

So much for the characteristics of the black soul, the
négritude of the West African. But there are also customs
and institutions which African writers, whether of the
West or the East, believe to be characteristic of their
societies, either now or in a legendary past when values
had not been demoralized by colonial rule. It is worth
asking what these cultural characteristics are, that they
should be picked out by men as diverse as Blyden,
Césaire, Diop, Senghor, Nkrumah, Abraham, and Nyerere. First, all seem to agree that traditional Africa was
remarkable for its sense of brotherhood and mutual
help. Blyden writes of the fundamental community of
African life, the mutual help, the community in land
and absence of "individualistic competition."[28] Diop
speaks of "the love and the sense of brotherhood that are
the cardinal virtues of the negro." Césaire claims that
Africans originally had communal institutions, and
Fontaine finds characteristic their collectivism and shar-
ing of labour in common.[29] Kenyatta and Nyerere also
write of the community spirit of Africans, and it accords
with many of their political and economic objectives.
Nyerere addressing a TANU meeting in 1966 said that
"in traditional Africa the people were equal; they co-
operated together and they participated in the decisions
which affected their life."[30]

Mutual help is of course characteristic of small, isolated, rural communities all over the world. It is their
form of social insurance in time of disaster: "You help

[28] July, p. 215.
[29] W. T. Fontaine, "Philosophical Aspects of Contemporary African
Social Thought," in *Pan-Africanism Reconsidered*, p. 246.
[30] Julius Nyerere, *Presidential Address to the National Congress of
TANU* (Dar-es-Salaam: Ministry of Information and Tourism, October,
1967), p. 15.

me when wild pigs have rooted up my crops and I will
help you when it is your turn to suffer." More specially
characteristic of Bantu, Nilotic, and Negro societies is
the variety of corporate kinship groups based on uni-
lineal descent and the basic role they play in economic,
political, and religious life, a characteristic not mentioned by the Pan-Africanists. Interesting, too, are the
many forms of joint ownership of land and other
property combined with family and individual claims,
in other words, not "love and the sense of brotherhood"
but the acceptance of a very heterogeneous bundle of
rights. The sense of equality of the individual varies
greatly from society to society in Africa. It was small in
the case of some of the centralized kingdoms like the
Akan states or Buganda and much greater in the age-set
societies of East Africa. Participation in the decisions
which affected their life was certainly a characteristic.
Moreover, joint ownerships, mutual self-help, and the
virtues of small community life are bound to be threatened by industrialization. Some African politicians, and
perhaps Nyerere is one of them, speak with the same
nostalgia for past days that English villagers have when
they watch the break-up of their social life. Old people
in the Essex village where I live tell me that "Everyone
helped each other in the old days" or "People were
kinder." The words are strangely familiar to a student of
Pan-African literature.

There are other African traits on which our writers
seem to be agreed. They include a strong sense of religion, with an emphasis on ancestor worship, and a sense
of identity with nature. Césaire speaks of respect for life
and an African sense of integration with the cosmos;[31]
and Carter, in a study of traditional African social think-

[31] Fontaine, p. 247.

ing, claims that the belief that the social and natural orders of the world are linked is a specially African contribution to thought.[32] It is also surely a characteristic of the thought of Shakespearian England!

The list of common features is in fact a short one. It does not include, curiously enough, the elaboration of political forms which fascinates the anthropologist making comparative studies in Africa, or the variety of different councils with executive and judicial functions which are such a marked feature of African, as distinct from many other preindustrial societies, or the unusual development of their legal institutions. Perhaps this is because the Pan-Africanists as a whole wish to forget the different tribal polities by which Africa is inhabited, and their own as well. Nkrumah, of course, wrote as though the colonial powers had invented ethnic differences, although he cannot have believed this to be true. Colonial boundaries were certainly drawn arbitrarily and many of them cut in half peoples of the same culture and speaking the same language. This was done, for instance, by the northern boundary of Uganda or the old division between the British and French Cameroons. On these grounds, Nkrumah was no doubt justified in his statement that "We were chopped into bits and pieces." But his assumption that Africa was once united and was, in his words, "a historical people," and that it was then divided into "colonies," obviously flies in the face of every known historical fact. In reality, the colonial territories often made possible the largest and most permanent grouping of peoples which had ever existed in the continent, except perhaps in the case of Egypt. Once colonial boundaries had been fixed, it is perfectly true

[32] George Carter, "Traditional African Social Thought," in *Pan-Africanism Reconsidered*, p. 257.

that political units of different types were created and
that English, French, or Portuguese began to be the
languages of government and education. Further cooperation no doubt became harder. But even if Africa
had been administered by a metropolitan power with a
single language, it would still show the same diversity of
indigenous cultures it has now.

These then were the main alternatives by which a
Europeanized élite tried to solve some of their emotional
and political difficulties. Africans were inferior in culture but could be raised to the level of Europeans. Africans were once superior in civilization and could become
so again. Africans have something unique, different,
superior, and in keeping with Pan-African ideals of a
single United States of Africa. None of these solutions
to the problem seems likely to be permanent: too many
contradictions are involved. For the élite, the concept
of a united Africa will surely be much more securely
based on the common experiences of African leaders in
newly independent countries than on myths of the existence of a single culture. The fight against colonialism
may be forgotten before long. The period was a very
short one in terms of East African history. It will depend
how far this fight is used as a unifying myth in teaching
history in the African schools. But the experience of
nation-building in a hurry is certainly a unifying factor.
Never before have groups of young men been able to
form and reform their constitutions so quickly and to
draw on the political institutions of the world for their
models.

The experience of thrashing out the concept of African socialism is another field of endeavour on which
African leaders also share notes. There is a pride in the

African states' claim to nonalignment and in their concept of the Third World, called into being, some Africans hope, to redress the balance between the two great hostile superpowers. Certainly by the system of representation at the United Nations, Africans wield a power quite out of proportion to their often tiny populations.

In other words, for the élite the common experiences of the new states may take the place of those based on the study of the past. This is a line which has been taken in many of the French states, territories in which the élite has always lived much more apart from the ordinary peasant than in the British territories. J. Ki-Zerbo of the Republic of the Upper Volta evidently expresses this view when he writes that "the African personality of which the whole world is speaking will be what the African people make it."[33]

The work of the new African universities is already beginning to break down the intellectuals' fear of tribal differences. African studies, in the form of African history, sociology, anthropology, the economic history of African territories, and political science as applied to African governments are established in all the three East African University colleges—Makerere at Kampala, the Royal College at Nairobi, and the University College of Tanzania at Dar-es-Salaam.

With the big expansion of African universities after World War II, it was impossible to provide this teaching immediately. Textbooks did not exist. Expatriate teachers recruited in large numbers were too overburdened with teaching to undertake local research and did not

[33] J. Ki-Zerbo, "African Personality and the New African Society," in *Pan-Africanism Reconsidered*, p. 267. The study of African jurisprudence has so far lagged behind although it is now being developed at the University of Tanzania.

immediately see the need for it. African students were still suspicious that special teaching on African problems meant inferior teaching.

The East African Institute of Social Research set up at Makerere in 1950 was one of the centres established under the Colonial Social Science Research Council to bridge this gap. When it started its work, research in African history had hardly begun; modern studies of the major ethnic groups in the East African region had not been undertaken; economic histories of different areas and the major crops were lacking. Now the position has changed. African studies centres exist at all East African universities. An African student who has done research on some piece of local African history naturally begins to find the myth of the single African culture uninteresting compared with the complexity of the situation which his work reveals. The history of colonial penetration in particular districts and subdistricts has been found a most rewarding subject of research. In 1952, anthropologists of the East African Institute of Social Research produced a study of the basis of selection of chiefs in fourteen tribes in the area; and this led, among other things, to generalizations as to the reactions of African societies of different types to British rule and indeed to centralized rule in general.[34] Tribal differences were here the subject of research in the political-administrative field; they were to be sought out and evaluated, and not obliterated.

The University of Syracuse research project on rural development described in Chapter III produced a series of community studies showing the part played by traditional authorities, such as elders or councils in community schemes. Here again it is differences, and often small differences, in local institutional arrangements which account for the differential reactions of a series of societies to new plans for better living. Field research is surely bound to make the study of tribal differences a matter of fascination rather than a subject to be perpetually tabooed. The telescope will be lowered from the blind eye!

This is, I am sure, the way to advance. If African states want a culture of their own, they must cease to be afraid of their diverse origins and rejoice in the very richness of this diversity, and try to incorporate many elements boldly in their educational programmes and local government policies. "Africa needs a constant reminder of its massively traditional nature and its best prospects lie in utilising this tradition and heritage."[35] East African scholars with their newer traditions and greater freedom from the classical curricula of nineteenth-century Europe may well have the best chance of experimenting successfully in these directions.

34 Audrey I. Richards, ed., *East African Chiefs* (London: Faber & Faber, 1960).
35 Abraham, p. 188.

BIBLIOGRAPHY

General

Abraham, W. E. *The Mind of the African.* The Nature and Human Society Series. London: Weidenfeld and Nicolson, 1961.

Allan, William. *The African Husbandman.* London: Oliver and Boyd, 1965.

Almond, Gabriel A., and Coleman, James S. *The Politics of Developing Areas.* Princeton: Princeton University Press, 1960.

American Society of African Culture. *Pan-Africanism Reconsidered.* Berkeley and Los Angeles: University of California Press, 1962.

Ashby, Sir Eric. *African Universities and Western Tradition.* The Godkin Lectures, Harvard University, 1964. London: Oxford University Press, 1964.

Banks, Arthur Leslie, ed. *The Development of Tropical and Sub-Tropical Countries, with Particular Reference to Africa.* London: Arnold, 1954.

Biebuyck, Daniel, ed. *African Agricultural Systems.* London: Oxford University Press for the International African Institute, 1963.

Carter, Gwen, ed. *African One-Party States.* Ithaca: Cornell University Press, 1962.

Dumont, René. *L'Afrique noire est mal partie.* Collections esprit "Frontière Ouverte." Paris: Editions du Seuil, 1962.

———. *False Start in Africa.* Translated by Phyllis Nauts Ott. London: André Deutsch, 1966.

Fallers, Lloyd A. "Equality, Modernity and Democracy in the New States." In *Old Societies and New States,* edited by Clifford Geertz. New York: Free Press of Glencoe, 1963.

Firth, Raymond W., ed. *Themes in Economic Anthropology.* London: Tavistock Publications, 1967.

———. and Yamey, B. S. *Capital, Saving and Credit in Peasant Societies.* London: Allen and Unwin, 1964.

Forde, C. Daryll, ed. *African Worlds; Studies in the Cosmological Ideas and Social Values of African Peoples.* London: Oxford University Press for the International African Institute, 1954.

Fortes, Meyer, and Evans-Pritchard, E. E., eds. *African Political Systems*. London: Oxford University Press for the International African Institute, 1940.

Geertz, Clifford, ed. *Old Societies and New States; the Quest for Modernity in Asia and Africa*. New York: Free Press of Glencoe, 1963.

Great Britain. Colonial Office. *Report of the Commission on Closer Union of the Dependencies in Eastern and Central Africa* (Hilton-Young Commission). Cmd. 3234. London: HMSO, 1929.

——. *Memorandum on Mass Education in Africa*, Col. No. 186. London: HMSO, 1943.

Gutkind, Peter C. W. "Urban Conditions in Africa." *The Town Planning Review*, 32, No. 1 (1961): 20-32.

Hailey, Lord Malcolm. *An African Survey; A Study of Problems Arising in Africa South of the Sahara*. London: Oxford University Press for the Committee of the African Research Survey, 1938.

——. *An African Survey*. Rev. ed. London: Oxford University Press, 1957.

Hodgkin, Thomas L. *Nationalism in Colonial Africa*. London: Muller, 1956.

Hunter, Guy. *The Best of Both Worlds?* London: Oxford University Press for the Institute of Race Relations, 1967.

International African Institute. *Ethnographic Survey of Africa*. Vol. 1. London, New York: Oxford University Press, 1950—.

July, Robert William. *The Origins of Modern African Thought*. London: Faber & Faber, 1967.

Lee, J. M. *Colonial Government and Good Government*. Oxford: Clarendon Press, 1967.

Mair, Lucy P. *Primitive Government*. Middlesex: Penguin Books, 1962.

Schapera, Isaac, *Government and Politics in Tribal Societies*. London: Watts, 1956.

Seligman, Charles Gabriel. *The Races of Africa*. N.p.: Home University Library of Modern Knowledge, 1930.

Worsley, Peter. *The Third World*. The Nature of Human Society Series. London: Weidenfeld and Nicolson, 1964.

General East African Literature

Diamond, Stanley, and Burke, Fred G. *The Transformation of East Africa*. New York: Basic Books for the Program of East African Studies, University of Syracuse, 1966.

Great Britain. Colonial Office. *East Africa:Report of the Economic and Fiscal Commission.* Sir Jeremy Raisman, Chairman (Raisman Report). Cmnd. 1279. London: HMSO, 1961.

——. *Report of the East Africa Commission, 1925.* Cmd. 2387. London: HMSO, 1925.

——. *Joint Select Committee on East Africa.* Minutes of Evidence. London: HMSO, 1931.

Great Britain. Secretary of State. *Despatch on Local Government.* Colonial Despatch, February 25, 1947.

East African Common Services Organization. East African Statistical Department. *Quarterly Economic and Statistical Review.* Nairobi: Government Printer, June, 1964.

Ingham, Kenneth. *A History of East Africa.* London: Longmans, Green, 1962.

Richards, Audrey I., ed. *East African Chiefs.* London: Faber & Faber, 1960.

Speke, John Hanning. *Journal of the Discovery of the Source of the Nile.* Edinburgh and London: Blackwood and Sons, 1863.

Stanley, Sir Henry Morton. *Through the Dark Continent.* Vol. I. New York: Harpers, 1878.

Kenya

Fearn, Hugh. *An African Economy; A Study of the Economic Development of the Nyanza Province of Kenya 1903-53.* London: Oxford University Press for the East African Institute of Social Research, 1961.

Huxley, Elspeth Joscelin. *A New Earth; An Experiment in Colonialism.* London: Chatto & Windus, 1960.

International Bank for Reconstruction and Development. *The Economic Development of Kenya.* Baltimore: Johns Hopkins Press, 1963.

Kenya. Ministry for Economic Planning and Development. *Kenya Development Plan for 1965-66 to 1969-70.* Nairobi: Government Printer, 1966.

Kenyatta, Jomo. *African Socialism and its Application to Planning in Kenya.* Nairobi: Government Printer, 1965.

Swynnerton, R. T. M. *A Plan to Intensify the Development of African Agriculture in Kenya.* Nairobi: Government Printer, 1954.

Tanzania (Tanganyika)

Bennett, George. *An Outline History of TANU.* Reprint Series, No. 31. Oxford: Oxford Institute of Commonwealth Studies, 1963.

Fisher, Carol. "Tanzania Settlement." *Venture* 19, No. 6. London: Fabian Colonial Bureau, 1967.

International Bank for Reconstruction and Development. *The Economic Development of Tanganyika.* Baltimore: Johns Hopkins Press, 1961.

Nyerere, Julius. *The Arusha Declaration.* Dar-es-Salaam: Government Printer, 1967.

——. *Democracy and the Party System.* Dar-es-Salaam: Tanganyika Standard Limited, n.d.

——. *Presidential Address to the National Congress of TANU.* Dar-es-Salaam: Ministry of Information and Tourism, October 1967.

——. "*Ujamaa,* The Basis of African Socialism." TANU publication, 1962. Reprinted in *Freedom and Unity (Uhuru na Umoja).* London: Oxford University Press, 1967.

Rural Development Seminar at Dar-es-Salaam, April 1966. Mimeographed. Dar-es-Salaam: Tanzania Ministry of Information and Tourism, 1966.

Tanganyika. Laws of Tanganyika. *Native Authorities Ordinance, 1926.* Cap. 47, 1928.

Tanzania. Commission on Agricultural Development. *Report.* Dar-es-Salaam: Government Printer, 1965.

Taylor, James Clagett. *The Political Development of Tanganyika.* Stanford: Stanford University Press, 1963.

The United Republic of Tanganyika and Zanzibar. *Five-Year Plan for Economic and Social Development, July 1964-June 1969.*

Uganda

Apter, David. *The Political Kingdom in Uganda; A Study in Bureaucratic Nationalism.* Princeton: Princeton University Press, 1961.

Beattie, John H. M. *Bunyoro: An African Kingdom.* Case Studies in Cultural Anthropology. New York: Henry Holt, 1960.

Buganda Planning Commission Report. Kampala: Government Printer, 1965.

Burke, Fred G. *Local Government and Politics in Uganda.* Syracuse: Syracuse University Press, 1964.

Clark, Ralph. "Programmes and Policies." In *Aid in Uganda.* Part II. Edited by the Overseas Development Institute. London: The Institute, 1966.

Fallers, Lloyd A. *Bantu Bureaucracy.* Cambridge, England: W. Heffer for the East African Institute of Social Research, 1956.

——, ed. *The King's Men*. London: Oxford University Press for the East African Institute of Social Research, 1964.

Great Britain. Colonial Office. *Inquiry into African Local Government in the Protectorate of Uganda*. (Wallis Report). Entebbe: Government Printer, 1953.

——. *Report of the Constitutional Committee*. (Wild Report). Entebbe: Government Printer, 1959.

——. *Report of the Uganda Independence Conference, 1962*. Rt. Hon. Reginald Maudling, M.P., Chairman. Cmd. 1778. London: HMSO, June 29, 1962.

——. Uganda Relations Commission. *Report of the Uganda Constitutional Conference and Agreed Draft of New Buganda Agreement*. (Munster Report). Entebbe: Government Printer, 1961.

Harmsworth, J. "Peasant Agriculture: Labour Organisation in Four Selected Areas in East Uganda." Conference Paper, July 1962. Kampala: East African Institute of Social Research, 1962.

Ingham, Kenneth. *The Making of Modern Uganda*. London: Allen and Unwin, 1958.

International Bank for Reconstruction and Development. *The Economic Development of Uganda*. Baltimore: Johns Hopkins Press, 1962.

Kagwa, Sir Apolo. *Ekitabo kye Mpisa za Buganda*. ["The Customs of the Baganda in the Luganda Language"]. 1st ed. 1905. Kampala: Uganda Society, 1952.

Low, D. Anthony. *Political Parties in Uganda, 1949-62*. London Institute of Commonwealth Studies (Commonwealth Paper, No. 8). London: Athlone Press, 1962.

——, and Pratt, R. C. *Buganda and British Overrule*. London: Oxford University Press, 1960.

Morris, H. S. *The Indians in Uganda*. Chicago: University of Chicago Press, 1968.

Thomas, Harold B., and Scott, Robert. *Uganda*. London: Oxford University Press, 1935.

Uganda. Uganda Agricultural Department. *Record of Investigations*. No. 1. (J. H. Jameson). Entebbe: Government Printer, 1950.

——. Uganda Planning Commission. *Work for Progress: The Second Five-Year Plan, 1966-71*. Entebbe: Government Printer, 1966.

Wrigley, C. C. "The Changing Economic Structure of Buganda." In *The King's Men*. Edited by Lloyd A. Fallers. London: Oxford University Press, 1964.

———. *Crops and Wealth in Uganda.* East African Studies, No. 12. Kampala: East African Institute of Social Research, 1959.

Other Areas

Biebuyck, Daniel, and Douglas, Mary. *Congo Tribes and Parties.* RAI Pamphlet, No. 1. London: Royal Anthropological Institute, 1961.

Chambers, Robert. *New Society, the Social Science Weekly.* London: October 13, 1966.

Gaitskell, Arthur. *Gezira: A Story of Development in the Sudan.* Colonial and Comparative Studies. London: Faber & Faber, 1959.

Lewis, W. Arthur. *Politics in West Africa.* The Whidden Lectures, McMaster University, Hamilton, Ontario. London: Allen and Unwin, 1965.

Nkrumah, Kwame. Address to Congress of Africanists, Accra, 1963. *Présence Africaine* 17, No. 45 (1963): 5-18.

Perham, Margery F. *Native Administration in Nigeria.* London: Oxford University Press, 1937.

Smith, Michael G. *The Plural Society in the British West Indies.* Berkeley: University of California Press, 1965.

Wilkes, Ivor. "Aspects in Bureaucratization in Ashanti in the Nineteenth Century." *Journal of African History* 7, No. 2 (1966): 215-32.

INDEX

Kingdoms, 4, 6-7, 12, 23, 40, 42, 48-49, 51, 88-89, 93, 98, 106
Kings, 2, 4, 13, 18, 20, 23, 40, 42-43, 45, 48, 50-52, 68
Kuman, 41, 44

Labour, 2, 29, 103, 105; migration of, 46
Land, 57-58, 61, 63-64, 66, 77, 80; attitude to, 15, 26, 28, 57, 58; tenure, v, 14-15, 23, 57-58, 64, 70, 103, 105-6
Lango, 17, 34, 39, 41, 44, 50
Language, vi, 1, 7-8, 11, 13-14, 20, 22, 40-41, 44, 103, 107-8
Liberia, 84, 99, 101-2
Literacy, 12, 17, 33, 65, 71, 73, 88
Lobengula, 4
Local government, vi, 19, 23, 32, 45-46, 76, 111. *See also* Administration, local
Lonsdale, 2
Luganda, 10-11, 44, 50
Lugard, Lord, 16, 18, 44, 49
Lugbara, 41
Lumumba, Patrice, 38
Luo, 36-37

Malawi, 24, 59 (Table 5), 92
Mali, 88
Masai, 4, 8, 18, 69
Mau Mau, 63
Mboya, Tom, 93
Missionaries, 13, 24, 27, 32, 45, 78, 99
Molson Commission (1962), 49
Moshesh, 4
Mouvement National Congolais (MNC), 38
Munster Commission, 49
Mutesa I, 43-45
Mutesa II, 34, 43, 51

National assemblies, 11, 30, 32, 35, 38, 51, 85
National Council for Nigeria and the Cameroons (NCNC), 38
Native authorities, 15, 20, 23, 30-31, 66, 68-69
Négritude, 103-5
Nigeria, 3-4, 7-8, 18, 35, 38, 65, 97
Nilo-Hamitic, 8, 11, 19, 40-41
Nilotic, 4, 8-12, 19, 40-41, 106
Nkrumah, Kwame, 51-52, 88-89, 96, 98, 100-102, 105, 107
Northern People's Congress (NPC), 38
Nyerere, Julius, 77-80, 87, 92, 96, 105-6
Nyoro, 39, 42-44

Obote, Milton, 11, 34, 49-53, 87
O'cheng, 11
Odinga, Oginga, 11
Organization of African Unity (OAU), 93, 96-97

Padmore, George, 94
Pan-African Freedom Movement of East, Central and South Africa (PAFMECSA), 92-93, 96-97
Pan-Africanism, 84, 94-98, 106-8
Political leadership, 10-11, 16, 33, 38, 40, 57, 61, 64, 72-73, 76, 80, 83, 85, 88, 90-93, 97, 98-104, 106, 108
Political parties, vi, 29, 33, 36-38, 50, 72-73, 76, 85, 87
Political structure, 2-5, 11-13, 16, 18, 20, 26-27, 29, 42, 106-7
Présence Africaine, 26, 94, 97-99, 102-4, 109

Uhuru (freedom), 86-87
Umoja (unity), 87
United States, 16, 32, 74-75, 84-85, 94-99, 109
University, 11, 24, 31, 46, 48, 73, 89, 97, 100-101, 109; African Studies, 3, 101-4, 107-10; Liberia College, 101; Makerere University College, vi, 24, 31-32, 109-10; Royal College at Nairobi, 24, 109; University of Tanzania, 24, 81, 109
University of Syracuse, vii, 81, 110

Urundi, 46

Village, 7, 11, 22-25, 54, 62, 64-65, 68, 70, 73-75, 81-82; headman of, 15, 18, 67-68, 70-71. *See also* Administration, traditional

West Indies, 26, 29, 84, 94-96, 99
Wilde Commission (1959), 48

Yoruba, 3, 7, 38

Zambia, vi, 6, 24, 64, 70, 92
Zanzibar. *See* Tanzania